CHRISTIAN LIVING SERIES

~ Volume 4 ~

Christian Living Series

~ Volume 4 ~

Spiritual NOURISHMENT

by His Grace Bishop Youanis

ST SHENOUDA'S MONASTERY
SYDNEY, AUSTRALIA
2013

Christian Living Series - Volume 4
SPIRITUAL NOURISHMENT

COPYRIGHT © 2013
St. Shenouda Monastery

ST SHENOUDA MONASTERY
8419 Putty Rd,
Putty, NSW, 2330
Sydney, Australia

www.stshenoudamonastery.org.au

ISBN 13: 978-0-9873400-5-4

Cover Design:
Hani Ghaly,
Begoury Graphics
begourygraphics@gmail.com

Contents

The Holy Bible

𝒳

"Receive with meekness the implanted word, which is able to save your souls."
(James 1:21)

- ❧ The Book of God
- ❧ Blessings of the Book
- ❧ The Word in the life of God's men
- ❧ The place of the Holy Book in our reading
- ❧ Why do we study the Bible
- ❧ How do we study the Word of God
- ❧ Ways to study the Book
- ❧ The Coptic Church and the Book

THE BOOK OF GOD

Although there are many publications and books that are published every day with the aim of presenting human knowledge, the Holy Bible is still the number one Book, for it is truly the Book of God.

The Holy Scripture was not named as such by a person but it is the name given by the Holy Spirit, "and that from childhood you have known the Holy Scriptures, which are able to make you wise for salvation through faith which is in Christ Jesus." (2 Tim 3:15); "The Gospel of God which He promised before through His prophets in the Holy Scriptures." (Rom 1:1,2) Without a doubt, this name differentiates between the message of God in the Holy Book and other books written by Man in various divisions of knowledge.

The Holy Scripture is the Book of God from its beginning to its end. It consists of different books that were written by different people like Moses, David, Solomon, Matthew, Luke or Paul; however it was not their personal writing for the writer of the entire Bible is the Holy Spirit, the Spirit of God. "For prophecy never came by the will of man, but holy men of God spoke as they were moved by the Holy Spirit." (2 Peter 1:21) Furthermore, St Paul adds: "All Scripture is given by inspiration of God." (2 Tim 3:16) Those who studied the Bible closely in an attempt to discredit the Book, either were attracted to it and became believers or were destroyed!!

The Holy Scripture consists of two covenants, the Old and the New. The word covenant refers to the agreement between God and His people, both of which were sealed by blood, one with the blood of animal sacrifices, and the latter with Jesus' blood.

THE UNITY OF THE BOOK AND ITS AIM:

The Holy Bible is truly an amazing Book. It consists of 73 Books (46 in the Old Testament and 27 in the New Testament). It was written over 1500 years. Around 40 writers from different time periods and backgrounds participated in its writing. These include King David and King Solomon, a shepherd like Amos, a priest like Zechariah, a prophet like Samuel and Isaiah, Moses, a leader like Joshua, and fishermen like Peter and John. It was written in different places: Sinai desert, Judea's desert, a cave, a prison in Rome, Patmos Island, a palace in Zion, the riverside of Babel, Jerusalem after its reconstruction. Despite all the differences in personalities, locations and times of its writing, the 73 Books are united in One Book. One in its Spirit, its subject, and its aim and there is nothing strange about this because:

1. The core of the Book from the beginning to the end is "Jesus Christ the Son of God." At the beginning of the Holy Book, it announces that He shall bruise the head of the serpent "the devil." (Gen 3:15) At the end of the Book of Revelation, we read that He is coming soon "Surely I am coming quickly." (Rev 22:20) The Lord Jesus stressed this fact to the Jews by saying: "You search the Scriptures, for

in them you think you have eternal life; and these are they which testify of Me." (John 5:39) After His resurrection, He explained to Emmaus' disciples "And beginning at Moses and all the Prophets, He expounded to them in all the Scriptures the things concerning Himself." (Luke 24:27)

2. The main issue of the Book is God's relationship with man. The story of God in the entire Book is His love to man and His revelation so that man renews his hope. The Lord called Adam after he sinned and said "Where are you?" (Gen 3:9) Man hides from God but God searches for him and shows him the way of salvation.

God in the Holy Bible is different from other religions. For in other religions, man tries to reach God, but in Christianity, God reaches man. Man is a weak sinful person, and it is impossible that he can reach the Holy God by his/her endeavours alone.

3. The Holy Book teaches us that the Grace of God does not reach us directly but through an Intercessor. It teaches us that to obtain forgiveness of our sins, there must be intercession. This idea is mentioned throughout the Book. The Old Testament is full of prophecies about the Messiah "For there is one God and one Mediator between God and men, the Man Christ Jesus." (1 Tim 2:5) The Gospels show the Messiah living and working and the Epistles look towards Him and expect His Second coming through faith. Revelation talks about His authority and eternal kingdom.

THE EVERLASTING BOOK:

The Holy Book affects those who read it faithfully and humbly. It obliges many who read it to leave their sins. For real believers, the Book is like Samson in his strength, but for unbelievers, it is like Samson after having cut his hair and after having lost his strength.

Though the Bible has been translated in about 850 languages, it has not lost its strength or effect as its strength is not due to linguistic beauty but to the spirit in its words. The Lord Jesus said: "The words that I speak to you are spirit, and they are life." (John 6:63) It was able to attract millions to repentance and grant them joy, peace, and hope. It is a living Book with strong positive effects on those who read it through faith.

Voltaire, the French writer in the 18th century, said that he alone will oppose the Holy Bible and it will be forgotten in a hundred years. Well, many hundred years passed and nothing of what Voltaire said has happened; on the contrary the scientific opposition that was directed against the Holy Bible in the 18th and 19th century resulted in a more precise study of the Holy Bible. Through modern discoveries and archaeological studies, the truth of the Book was proved beyond all doubt.

The Holy Book will continue as an everlasting Book and not one letter will fall. The Lord said: "For assuredly I say to you, till heaven and earth pass away, one jot or one title will by no means pass from the law till all is fulfilled." (Matt 5:18); "Heaven and earth will pass away, but My words will by no means pass away." (Mark 13:31); (Rev 22:18-19).

BLESSINGS OF THE HOLY BOOK

The Word of God has countless blessings. We did not read about a person who led a holy spiritual life without the influence of the Holy Bible. We did not hear about an honest servant or a successful missionary worker or a struggling hero of faith who did not have the Holy Bible as his source of success, support and strength. God ordered that the two tablets, that were written on them the Ten Commandments, be placed in the Tabernacle where the Manna was also preserved. No doubt this was a symbol. The heart which keeps the Word of God, is the heart in which the real Manna, Jesus Christ, also dwells.

We all know that Paradise was our original dwelling place but the original sin resulted in the expulsion of human kind from Paradise. The world we live in, is a foreign land where humanity is in constant war with evil spiritual enemies. In the Bible, the Lord very clearly explains that our support against these enemies is the Word of God. The Word of God is:

GOOD NEWS, HOPE AND COMFORT:

All human beings are sentenced to die as a result of their disobedience, but the Holy Bible proclaims good News to everyone. It proclaims life and freedom, sonship and release from slavery. It proclaims the blessings of the Cross and Resurrection and announces a better life and a Godly union. What a beautiful message received from the Holy Bible: "How beautiful are the feet of those who preach the gospel of peace, which bring glad tidings of good things!" (Rom 10:15)

Every fifty years, the Jews used to celebrate the year of Jubilee. It was a great celebration according to the Law. When the trumpets were blown announcing the year of Jubilee, everyone was happy for the poor man who was forced to sell his house or field would get it back and the person who had to sell himself as a slave would be free. (Lev 25) For this reason, the Psalmist blessed the people, "Blessed are the people who know the joyful sound!" (Psalm 89:15) The joyful sound was the trumpet announcing the beginning of the new Jubilee.

The Holy Bible is a Godly trumpet as it "[Proclaims] the acceptable year of the LORD." (Luke 4:19) It explains how we retrieved our heavenly home after we lost it to sin and disobedience. It explains how we became free after having enslaved ourselves by sin and the spell of Satan.

The Holy Bible is not just good News about salvation and spiritual freedom as it also strengthens our hope and lifts our spirit. Spiritual enemies always spread weakness and defeat among the Lord's people, but the Holy Bible defeats these wicked thoughts and assumptions. The Holy Bible replaces these thoughts with faith, total submission to God, trust in His salvation, and the belief in His Coming to those who wait for Him.

Thus we read Moses' words to his people when they were frightened: "Do not be afraid. Stand still, and see the salvation of the LORD ... The LORD will fight for you, and you shall hold your peace." (Ex 14:13,14) We then read what the Lord did to his people in the wilderness for forty years, feeding them the food of the angels and giving them water from a rock, keeping their clothes and sandals without decay, and allowing them to conquer nations that were superior in both number and equipment. We also read about the wonderful work of God to his people everywhere and in every generation, and His numerous promises to them, "Because he has set his love upon Me, therefore I will deliver him; I will set him on high, because he has known My name. He shall call upon Me, and I will answer him; I will be with him in trouble; I will deliver him and honor him. With long life I will satisfy him, and show him My salvation." (Psalm 91:14-16) We read Jesus Christ's words "I am with you always, even to the end of the age." (Matt 28:20); and the experiences of St Paul: "If God is for us, who can be against us?" (Rom 8:31) and "I can do all things through Christ who strengthens me." (Phil 4:13) We also read about God's love to the sinners and this encourages and strengthens us to continue in the right way.

Because of life's many hardships, many stumble and leave the faith but the Lord gave us His Book to support us in this foreign world. (Matt 24:10) It is our strong and faithful companion during hard times. When we face troubles, we can be encouraged by the Word of God. In contrast, we can not find such encouragement and support from man, just like Job described "Miserable comforters." (Job 16:12)

The Word of God is the support for all men of God. David says: "Remember the word to Your servant, upon which You have caused me to hope... This is my comfort in my affliction... I remembered Your judgement of old, O LORD, and have comforted myself...Unless Your law had been my delight, I would then have perished in my affliction." (Psalm 119:49,50,52,92) St Paul explains this saying: "For whatever things were written before were written for our learning, that we through the patience and comfort of the Scriptures might have hope." (Rom 15:4) St Paul also encourages the faithful to use the Book, "Therefore comfort one another with these words." (1 Thess 4:18) Comfort is instituted because the words of the Holy Bible are written by the Holy Spirit, the "Comforter." (John 14:26)

LIGHT AND GUIDANCE:

The blessing of the Word of God first lies in its effect on repentance. St Peter's few words on the Pentecost resulted in 3,000 souls believing in Jesus Christ. (Acts 2) St Paul's words, while in prison, had an effect on Felix, though regretfully, he lost the opportunity and told Paul "Go away for now; when I have a convenient time I will call for you." (Acts 24:25) Also when the Ethiopian read the book of Isaiah, Philip explained its meaning and he believed. (Acts 8)

In Jeremiah, the Lord said, "Is not My word like a fire? And like a hammer that breaks the rock in pieces." (Jer 23:29) Just like fire softens iron, the Word of God softens hard hearts. Just as the hammer breaks rock, the Word of God has its effect on stony hearts that are hardened by sin.

Man is a foreigner in this earth, thus, he needs someone to lead and guide him. The Word of God led the

Israelites as a pillar of light. Likewise, the Word of God is accompanying us until we enter the heavenly Jerusalem. Just like the star guided the Kings "till it came and stood over where the young Child was," (Matt 2:9) so too, the Word of God guides us and leads us to Jesus. It will never wrong or mislead its followers. As the Psalmist says: "I am a stranger in the earth; do not hide your commandments from me." (Psalm 119:19). The Word of God is the best guide to the soul.

It warns us when we deviate from the right path "Your ears shall hear a word behind you, saying, this is the way, walk in it, whenever you turn to the right hand or whenever you turn to the left." (Is 30:21) It teaches us and instructs us: "For whatever things were written before were written for our learning, that we through the patience and comfort of the Scriptures might have hope." (Rom 15:4); "All Scripture is given by inspiration of God, and is profitable for doctrine, for reproof, for correction, for instruction in righteousness, that the man of God may be complete, thoroughly equipped for every good work." (2 Tim 3:16-17). It is not strange then when men of God talk about the law as the light and lamp: "Your word is a lamp to my feet and a light to my path." (Psalm 119:105) Solomon said: "For the commandment is a lamp, and the law a light." (Prov 6:23) Also, St Peter states: "We have the prophetic word confirmed, which you do well to heed as a light that shines in a dark place, until the day dawns and the morning star rises in your hearts." (2 Peter 1: 19)

For this reason, our church lights candles when the Gospel is read. St Iraneous, one of the 4th century fathers, comments: "The candles that are lit during the reading of the Gospel are not just a custom in the Eastern churches, but to express the joy of the Gospel, just like the wise virgins who had their lamps lit."

IT IS A WEAPON AND A SUPPORT:

The Word of God acts as a powerful weapon for those who live and experience it. The Lord Jesus left us an example to follow in 1 Peter 2:21. He used this weapon to fend off Satan when he tried to tempt Him, by replying each time with the Word of God: "It is written..." (Matt 4) Blessed is the man who memorises the Word of God for it is converted into power. He will not be frightened to face the enemy, like when David faced Goliath.

St Paul says: "For the word of God is living and powerful, and sharper than any two-edged sword, piercing even to the division of soul and spirit, and of joints and marrow, and is a discerner of the thoughts and intents of the heart." (Heb 4:12) It penetrates the heart, reveals all evil thoughts and purifies it. The power of the Word lies, as St Athanasius explained, in that the Lord lives in His words.

When St Paul recommended that the Ephesians wear the "whole armour of God" to be able to defeat Satan, he mentioned different kinds of weapons; for he talked about the breastplate of righteousness, the shield of faith and the helmet of salvation. Though all these weapons are used in war, they all have a protective function. Then the apostle wrote about the strong positive weapon "the sword of the Spirit, which is the word of God." (Eph 6:10-17) The Word of God is like a sword with which the soldier can defeat his enemy.

The Word of God supports us in our spiritual struggle and helps the soul; "The law of the LORD is perfect, converting the soul." (Psalm 19:7) It also cleanses our deficiencies, as the Lord Jesus explained: "You are already clean because of the word which I have spoken to you." (John 15:3). It sanctifies the spirit: "Sanctify them by Your truth. Your word is truth." (John 17:17) Consequently, it thoroughly builds our spiritual life, "So now, brethren, I commend you to God and to the word of His grace, which is able to build you up and give you an inheritance among all those who are sanctified." (Acts 20:32). It can also save us: "Receive with meekness the implanted word, which is able to save your souls." (James 1:21)

The word of God is a bind for the mind, for when there are evil thoughts, the Word will awaken the mind, thus St Peter says: "Gird up the loins of your mind, be sober." (1 Peter 1:13) St Paul says: "Stand therefore, having girded your waist with truth" (Eph 6:14) and what is truth but the Word of God, "Your word is truth." (John 17:17)

When Joshua became a leader after the departure of Moses, the Lord commenced his work by telling him: "This Book of the Law shall not depart from your mouth, but you shall meditate in it day and night, that you may observe to do according to all that is written in it. For then you will make your way prosperous, and then you will have good success." (Josh 1:8) Therefore, the commandment was clear. Always remember the Word of God in order to be prosperous and successful.

The Psalmist begins: "Blessed is the man who walks not in the counsel of the ungodly...But his delight is in the law of the Lord, and in His law he meditates day and night. He shall be like a tree planted by the rivers of the water that brings forth its fruit in the season, whose leaf also shall not wither; and whatever he does shall prosper." (Psalm 1:1-3) This is a great description as the river of water represents the work of the Holy Spirit in the believers' heart. (John 7:38, 39)

IT IS THE MEASURE OF PERFECTION AND GROWTH:

Often a Christian deviates from the truth and is affected by society. As a result, his spiritual values change. He/she feels his life is good as long as he does not commit any major sins. But when one consults the Holy Bible, they read on how God asks us all to be perfect. One then identifies his/her faults. We should examine everything through the Word, "To the law and to the testimony! If they do not speak according to this word, it is because there is no light in them." (Is 8:20) The Jews in Piraeus, after listening to Paul and Silas preaching about Jesus, "received the word with all readiness, and searched the Scriptures daily to find out whether these things were so." (Acts 17:11) The Holy Bible is like a mirror to correct our spirit; it is a proper scale that reveals our heavy sins, so that we may repent. David said: "The law of the LORD is perfect, converting the soul." (Psalm 19:7). St Paul also said: "All Scripture is given by inspiration of God, and is profitable for doctrine, for reproof, for correction, for instruction in righteousness, that the man of God may be complete, thoroughly equipped for every good work." (2 Tim 3:16, 17)

When the Jews came to argue with Jesus, He told them: "He who is of God hears God's words; therefore you do not hear, because you are not of God." (John 8:47)

These words expound an important aspect in our spiritual life. We can measure our growth in grace by the extent of our love of the Word of God. If at any time we are not longing for the bread of life, we are sick spiritually. St John Chrysostom agrees to this when he said in one of his sermons: "When I see your desire to hear the holy teaching and observe you're longing to the spiritual bread which is God's Words, I clearly notice your growth in virtues. As we judge a healthy body when we observe one eating with pleasure, so we perceive your hunger to the Word of God as a sign of a healthy spiritual life."

THE HOLY BIBLE IN THE LIFE OF THE MEN OF GOD

We do not know of any holy men of God who did not rely on God's Word for spiritual growth. Any successful servant has the Word of God as the basis of his service. The Word of God has been and will always be the source of nourishment for all saints whether missionary, servants or faithful laymen. They memorise the Word of God and it preserves them. It is the Light that shines their way and makes them a light for others.

IN THE OLD TESTAMENT:

From the beginning, God emphasised the importance of the Word. He commanded Moses "And these words which I command you today shall be in your heart. You shall teach them diligently to your children, and shall talk of them when you sit in your house, when you walk by the way, when you lie down, and when you rise up. You shall bind them as a sign on your hand, and they shall be as frontlets between your eyes." (Deut 6:6-8) Shouldn't we examine these words and measure our love for the Word of God?

When God started working with Joshua, His first commandment was "This Book of the Law shall not depart from your mouth, but you shall meditate in it day and night, that you may observe to do according to all that is written in it. For then you will make your way prosperous, and then you will have good success." (Josh 1:8) This is a clear commandment. The Word of God must not depart from our mouth so that we can fulfil the will of God.

2. Relaxation of the body is a result of laziness, resting more than needed and taking too much sleep.

3. The illness of the body is any disorder in the glands which causes sexual rampage. This needs medical assistance. Body illness can also refer to the sensitivity of the sexual system as a result of practicing sin for a long time. Consequently, the body becomes very sensitive and is affected by any reason.

THE THOUGHTS

Referring to defiled thoughts which haunt a person and press the mind constantly.

This could be the result of an empty mind, i.e. nothing useful is occupying the mind. Sometimes this is a devilish war against pure saints. The devil uses it to defile the mind with lustful desires.

EXTERNAL REASONS

These are the stumbling blocks which come to us through our senses. The senses are the gates of information and the gates of stumble for a person. The eye sees exciting sights and the ear hears bad words. In both cases, sight and hearing are connected to the thought, and from here comes the sin.

1. The Sight:

The sight is a vital gate to youthful sins. Consequently, St Augustine considered it the first step of falling. This could be through looking lustfully at the other gender or looking through bad magazines, movies, television or reading obscene books that deal with sexual issues in the wrong manner.

2. Hearing:

This sense opens up your mind to dirty jokes and conversations from bad friends. Consequently, arousing bad thoughts and sexual desires.

3. Touch:

We can recognise the danger of this sense in an overcrowded place. It is also the direct reason for masturbation. Generally speaking, our presence at any place of sin will quickly reduce our spiritual resistance. If a piece of iron comes in contact with a magnetic orbit, it will get attracted and acquire the characteristics of the original magnet. There is no way the piece of iron can go back to its origin unless it escapes away from the magnetic orbit. Similarly, if we put ourselves in a bad orbit, as weak human beings, we will get attracted to it. We will not be able to return to our original purity unless we abandon this sinful atmosphere.

A Spiritual Elder says; "This is the order of the children of God's senses: Prevent your eyes from looking at human beauty, instead, look at God. Prevent your ears from hearing obscene words, instead, listen to the secrets of the Mighty. Beware of smelling bad aromas, and close your mouth in total awareness because this leads to total destruction. Preserve your tongue from void conversations as it is sufficient for you to talk to God, Your Creator. Finally, handle the fifth sense; which is touch; to the Vigilant Protector, ask for purity in all your movements so that the Lord might protect you from unclean thoughts".

OTHER REASONS

1. Most Dangerous Case:

The most dangerous case is when sexual feelings becomes a permanent desire inside the heart. The mind gets occupied with sexual pictures, imagines sexual situations and lives with that feeling all the time. Finally, he loses his simplicity and expects defilement in everything, even innocent incidents. The whole body becomes aroused and the mind is full of sexual thoughts and emotions.

Lord Jesus says, "But I say to you that whoever looks at a woman to lust for her has already committed adultery with her in his heart." (Matt. 5: 28) He didn't say, " whoever looks at a woman has already committed adultery with her." Therefore, the main issue in this sin is the desire; "Then, when desire has conceived, it gives birth to sin; and sin, when it is full-grown, brings forth death." (James 1: 15). There is great cooperation between the four sources of desire, whether through the heart, thought, senses or body. Wherever desire starts, it defiles the rest of the sources and so on.

The horrible fact about sexual sin, is that it consumes everything in a human being; his body, soul, mind and senses. Moreover, when someone sins sexually, his fall is a huge one and everything is destroyed within him. St Paul says, "Flee sexual immorality. Every sin that a man does is outside the body, but he who commits sexual immorality sins against his own body." (1 Cor. 6: 18)

2. Pride:

Someone might ask: What is the relationship between pride and adultery?

The answer is very clear: The Heavenly grace departs a proud person because of his pride. As a result, he falls in sin and the Lord allows this to happen so that he might feel weak and humiliated, thus regret his pride and humble himself. There is no greater sin which humiliates a spiritually proud person more than falling into adultery. Adultery is sometimes referred to as the sin of impurity because of its awfulness. St John of the Ladder says, "If you do not get rid of pride, you can never conquer adultery or any other sin." He also says, "No one ever conquered his body except he who humbled his heart, and no one ever humbled his heart except he who killed his desires." The early saintly fathers say: "The person who is proud of his asceticism falls into adultery, and he who is proud of being knowledgeable falls into blasphemy."

Adultery hides in pride while judgment protects it. Do not allow yourself to condemn or mock a person who falls into sexual sins, but have mercy and pray for him that the Lord might lift him up, and that his fall might be a reason for his humility. Always remember that you are a weak human being, at a risk of experiencing pains and temptations exactly like him. Tell yourself "He had fallen today, I might fall tomorrow." If you are a person who rushes into condemning and despising others, be sure that one day, God will teach you an unforgettable lesson, that is to discover your weakness. Maybe God will allow you to fall into the same sin. St Paul says, "Do not be haughty, but fear." (Rom. 11: 20)

Examine yourself, my dear; examine your spiritual path. Maybe your sexual desires are a result of your pride which caused the Divine grace to abandon you.

There are two vital issues related to sexuality: love and energy. Each person has the emotion of love. If this emotion is not directed properly, the devil can use it in sexual lust and desires. However, those who have satisfied this emotion correctly and spiritually are very comfortable when it comes to sexual issues. Some examples of satisfying the emotion of love in a proper manner:

1. Visiting the sick: Love here is shown in a caring sympathetic manner. It is very hard to get sexual fights while performing such a love.

2. Visiting the poor, widows and orphans: This may be in orphanages or other locations of social services.

3. Different spiritual services: such as calming those in hardships, comforting the grieving or visiting prisoners.

4. Tutoring: Such as serving in Sunday school classes and experiencing all the lovely feelings related to this service; parenting, care, love and friendship.

5. Friendships: An isolated person, who has no friends to exchange love and friendship, could easily fall into sexual fights, to make up for the lack of love inside his heart. So if you want to escape these fights, have good relationships

with faithful friends and protect yourself from sin.

6. Patriotic love and hobbies: Such as getting engaged in patriotic activities, writing poetry, playing music and all sorts of useful hobbies.

Each one has a certain level of energy and enthusiasm, and if it is not used in a useful way, one will certainly slip into harmful sexual desires. So a person, who uses his energy in playing sports or social service, will not face as much fights as a person who lives in relaxation and excessive bodily rest.

DIFFERENT STAGES OF SIN

Sexual issues go through different stages, depending on how severe or deep they are. Every stage needs an appropriate remedy. On the other hand, there are general tips which befit any of the following stages:

1. A fight from outside, while the heart is pure from inside.

2. A superficial response to sin, not thinking too much about it.

3. A severe indulgence through the mind, heart and senses. This is divided into two parts: one part is where sin is present and a person is ready to commit it. The second part is where sin is far and the person is trying hard to commit it.

4. The fourth stage is when sin becomes a habit.

As for David the prophet and King, all his Psalms are full of praise and love towards the Word of God. He says in one Psalm: "I delight to do Your will, O my God, and Your law is within my heart." (Psalm 40:8) In this expression, it is easy to see the great love that was present in David's heart for the Word of God. Let us also reflect on Psalm 119. This is a special Psalm and is the longest. In almost every verse, there is a word that reflects on the Holy Bible. For example: testimonies, commandments, statutes, law, and judgements. This psalm emphasises that the Word of God is Life to the believer.

It is his strength during his youth: "How can a young man cleanse his way? By taking heed according to Your word." (119: 8) It is the meditation of the believer, all day: "Oh, how I love Your law! It is my meditation all the day" (119: 97); and all night: "My eyes are awake through the night watches, that I may meditate on Your word." (119: 148) It is one's comfort forever: "You, through Your commandments, make me wiser than my enemies; for they are ever with me." (119: 98) The Word of God became the most precious thing to David as he says: "The law of Your mouth is better to me than thousands of coins of gold and silver." (119: 72); "Therefore I love Your commandments more than gold, yes, than fine gold!" (119: 127) He shows that studying the Word of God is an enjoyment: "I long for Your salvation, O Lord, and Your law is my delight." (119: 174). It gives him a new spirit: "I opened my mouth and panted, for I longed for Your commandments." (119:131)

Solomon also says: "My son, keep my words and treasure my commands within you. Keep my commands and live, and my law as the apple of your eye. Bind them

on your fingers; write them on the tablet of your heart."
(Prov 7:1-3) Jeremiah expresses his love of the Word by
saying: "Your words were found, and I ate them, and Your
word was to me the joy and rejoicing of my heart." (Jer
15:16) The Lord revealed to Ezekiel the strength of the
Word and its beauty, "Moreover He said to me, "Son of
man, eat what you find; eat this scroll, and go, speak to the
house of Israel." So I opened my mouth, and He caused me
to eat that scroll.

And He said to me, "Son of man, feed your belly, and
fill your stomach with this scroll that I give you." So I ate,
and it was in my mouth like honey in sweetness. Then He
said to me: "Son of man, go to the house of Israel and speak
with My words to them." (Ezek 3:1-4)

IN THE NEW TESTAMENT:

The Lord Jesus shows us the importance of the Word
when He sat with the teachers in the temple as a 12
year old, listening and asking them questions. When He
accepted to be tempted by Satan, He defeated him by the
strength of the Word. Every time, He answered saying, "It
is written..." clarifying that the Word of God is food for
the spirit. "Man shall not live by bread alone, but by every
word that proceeds from the mouth of God." (Matt 4:4)

It also serves as proof that we love Him: "If you love
Me, keep My commandments." (John 14:15) "The words
that I speak to you are spirit, and they are life." (John 6:63)
Not knowing the Word of God, creates delusions. The Lord
said this to the Jews: "You are mistaken, not knowing
the Scriptures nor the power of God." (Matt 22:29)

Furthermore, in the parable of Lazarus and the rich man, He explained that the Holy Books can save people. When the rich man asked Abraham to send Lazarus to his five brothers to help them, Abraham replied "They have Moses and the prophets; let them hear them.' And he said, 'No, father Abraham; but if one goes to them from the dead, they will repent.' But he said to him, 'If they do not hear Moses and the prophets, neither will they be persuaded though one rise from the dead.'" (Luke 16:27-31) Moreover, when a woman praised the Lord Jesus saying: "Blessed is the womb that bore You, and the breasts which nursed You," Jesus' reply was: "More than that, blessed are those who hear the word of God and keep it!"(Luke 11:27-28)

Christians were careful to teach their children the Word of God. St Paul mentioned that to Timothy, "and that from childhood you have known the Holy Scriptures, which are able to make you wise for salvation through faith which is in Christ Jesus." (2 Tim 3:15)

Youth become strong and steadfast by the Word, as St John the Beloved says: "I have written to you, young men, because you are strong and the word of God abides in you, and you have overcome the wicked one." (1 John 2:14) The Epistles are full of statements that show the importance of the Word of God. We have only mentioned a few here. Finally, we find that the Lord shows the importance of the Word in Revelation: "Blessed is he who reads and those who hear the words of this prophecy, and keep those things which are written in it." (Rev 1:3)

We find this evident in the lives of the saints of the church who studied the Holy Bible and memorised many parts of it. Not only did they memorise the Psalms, but also other books of the Bible. This proved that the Word of Jesus lived in them in abundance. (Col 3:16)

THE PLACE OF THE HOLY BIBLE IN OUR READINGS

There are many publications that are currently available, even though a person may not find the time to read them all. Although there are many books and magazines written about the Holy Bible, Theology, and history of the church, the Holy Bible excels them all. It is like the sun and everything else are like stars reflecting its light. Thus, it is not appropriate at any time to depend on these books, instead of the Holy Bible. There should be a specified time to read and study the Word of God. We are often mistaken when we read other books written by mere human beings, more than reading the Book of God. "Blessed is the man whom You instruct, O LORD, and teach out of Your law." (Psalm 94:12)

In the early years of Christianity, few people knew how to read. Often people would gather around someone who has the Holy Bible, or at least sections of it, and listen happily and thankfully to the Word of God, remembering the Lord's blessing: "Blessed is he who reads and those who hear the words of this prophecy, and keep those things which are written in it." (Rev 1:3)

Today the Holy Book is available to everyone and there are more people that can read than before, but unfortunately few choose to read it. The talent of reading is one of the most important talents of man today, so it is not good to stand in front of the Lord's throne one day, apologising for not using this precious talent to study His Word. If a friend sends you a letter, you would probably open it quickly to read his news and probably do this happily. What about the letters of our Holy Lord which are full of good news and joyful promises about the eternal life? We should be eager to know all its content. David expressed these feelings: "For I have chosen your precepts. I long for Your salvation, O LORD, and Your law is my delight." (Psalm 119:173,174) "Make me to hear joy and gladness that the bones You have broken may rejoice." (Psalm 51:8) No words carry the message of salvation more than the words of the Holy Bible.

Students should dedicate certain hours to meet their Teacher Jesus. His Word should be placed in front of anything else. You should give the Lord the early hours of the day for it is difficult to be attentive to the holy thoughts after our involvement in our daily tasks. The people of Israel had to pick up the manna when they were in the wilderness before sunrise or it would dissolve and disappear. Thus, we too should study the Word of God, early before breakfast, as we sit with the Lord alone, to pick our spiritual food, before walking in the wilderness of the world.

We acknowledge that studying the Word of God in the morning hour before breakfast may not be easy due to work or other circumstances. But God, being the Lover of mankind, knows of each one's condition and as long as he/she carries out this study at any other hour of the day, they will receive their reward just like those of the eleventh hour. (Matt 20:9) We also know that not everyone has equal availability to sit alone with God and His Holy Bible, but the Lord repeats the miracle of the manna as it is said:

"He who gathered much had nothing left over, and he who gathered little had no lack." (2 Cor 8:15) This means if we cannot dedicate a long time to the Lord, He will still bless and provide us with our "daily bread."

We have a duty towards our children, regarding the Word of God. The Lord commanded his children to teach His Words to their own children: "And these words which I command you today shall be in your heart. You shall teach them diligently to your children." (Deut 6:6-7) "Therefore you shall lay up these words of mine in your heart and in your soul, You shall teach them to your children." (Deut 11:18-19) Many honest parents followed God's commandment. In this, St Paul praised Timothy as he knew the Holy Books since his childhood, through the faith of his grandmother Lois and his mother Eunice. (2 Tim 1:5) Thus, we should read the Word of God to our children before they learn to read. We should encourage them to study the Holy Bible.

WHY SHOULD WE STUDY THE HOLY BIBLE?

There are many benefits in studying the Holy Bible:

IT IS THE BOOK OF SALVATION:

It is the Book that explains the salvation of humanity through our Saviour Jesus Christ. There is nothing more important than this matter: the forgiveness of our sins, our salvation, our victory and our eternal life. "Without shedding of blood, there is no remission." (Heb 9:22); "He who believes in the Son has everlasting life; and he who does not believe the Son shall not see life, but the wrath of God abides on him." (John 3:36); "Who is he who overcomes the world, but he who believes that Jesus is the Son of God?" (1 John 5:5)

The Old Testament recited how God dealt with His people and prophets. It recited His teachings and His commandments, and accordingly, we should base our behaviour, worship and faith. It also has many symbols and prophecies about the coming of Jesus. The New Testament tells us about the fulfilment of these prophecies, the life of Jesus on earth and His teachings for our new life.

Thus, the Holy Bible consists of one continuous topic, the story of humanity. That is the basis of our religion and the basis of eternal life and the happiness of mankind. The Almighty Lord taught the Jews who thought they knew the

Holy Books saying: "You search the Scriptures, for in them you think you have eternal life; and these are they which testify of Me. But you are not willing to come to Me that you may have life." (John 5:39-40) Jesus said to the Jews: "You think you have eternal life" for they used to study the Bible for the sake of the Law rather than the spirit.

As for us, let us search the Holy Scripture for it carries the message of salvation and is capable of leading us to the source of life, truth and eternity.

THE NOURISHMENT OF THE SPIRIT:

The body is nourished by physical food while the spirit is fed by spiritual food like prayer, studying the Word of God and partaking of the Holy Body and Blood. The daily food for the believer is prayer and the Word of God. When we pray, we talk to God and when we study the Word of God, He talks to us. These two spiritual nourishments are two electrical cords that link to the source of spiritual power, needed for our daily energy.

So what can happen to a person if he does not eat regularly? He will gradually become weak and may die. The same applies to the spirit. If it is not nourished, it will become weak and dry. We previously mentioned the blessings of the Holy Bible and how Satan deceives man into becoming careless with the Holy Bible. Soon after, the soul enslaves to Satan. David the Prophet experienced this when he said: "Unless Your law had been my delight, I would then have perished in my affliction." (Psalm 119:92)

When we eat, we do not see how the food is transformed into energy or tissue in our bodies but we feel the strength when we start to work. The same applies to our spiritual life. Our spiritual nourishment is converted into spiritual energy that is manifested when required. Blessed is he who nourishes his body and looks after the food of his spirit as the Lord said: "Man shall not live by bread alone, but by every word that proceeds from the mouth of God." (Matt 4:4)

THE LAW OF THE FINAL JUDGEMENT:

Although the Holy Bible is the Book of our Salvation and our spiritual food, it is also the law that will judge us and the entire world in the last days. The Lord Jesus said: "He who rejects Me, and does not receive My words, has that which judges him—the word that I have spoken will judge him in the last day." (John 12:48) St Paul said: "In the day when God will judge the secrets of men by Jesus Christ, according to my gospel." (Rom 2:16) Thus, if we will be judged by the Holy Book, we better know and live according to its commandments.

HOW DO WE STUDY THE WORD OF GOD?

WITH THE SPIRIT:

The Holy Bible is not an ordinary book produced by an ordinary person but it is the Book of God written by His Holy Spirit. A person may read a passage and find it just simply words, while another reads it and discovers amazing depth. Truly the Book is spiritually deep and has a hidden mystery behind its plain words.

A human eye can read the words of the Book and understand its direct meaning but few people can understand the true significance of the words of God. We need God to open our eyes so we can understand. That is why David asked the Lord: "Open my eyes, that I may see wondrous things from Your law;" (Psalm 119:18) "For the children of God were given to know the mysteries of the kingdom of heaven." (Matt 13:11).

When the soldiers of the King of Syria surrounded the city of Dotham to capture Elisha, his servant Gehazi was frightened and asked him what to do. The prophet calmed down his servant and prayed: "LORD, I pray, open his eyes that he may see." Then the LORD opened the eyes of the young man, and he saw. Behold, the mountain was full of horses and chariots of fire. (2 Kings 6: 17) Both Elisha and Gehazi are human with two eyes, but one could see while another could not. Elisha had his eyes spiritually opened.

There are many spiritual meanings and abundant

blessings in the Word of God, but we do not see it. We need the Lord to open our eyes. Every time we open the Bible, let us pray that the Lord may open our eyes to see the wondrous thing in His Law.

It is not easy to reach the depth of the Word of God. Many scientists, saints and monks spend all their lives studying the Bible but do not reach all its spiritual meaning. None of them have said that they have finished studying and understanding the Book. They felt that all their effort was just the beginning of a long journey. The Holy Bible was written for mankind to live by. Furthermore, the Spirit reveals to each one a certain aspect from it. David lived this and told the Lord: "I have seen the consummation of all perfection, but Your commandment is exceedingly broad." (Psalm 11:96) If David reached this conclusion, then what about us?

Thus, if we have a closer relation with the Lord and are keen to study His Book by the spirit, He will reveal to us new meanings. The Lord is ready to give us many blessings and uncover many of His secrets but we cannot grasp the Glory of God. That is why David said: "I will run the course of Your commandments, for You shall enlarge my heart." (Psalm 119:32) Accordingly, when we endeavour to learn God's commandments, He will enlarge our hearts, making them more sensitive to repentance. The following words of God will apply to us: "Every scribe instructed concerning the kingdom of heaven is like a householder who brings out of his treasure things new and old." (Matt 13:52)

This is what the Lord Jesus said: "The words that I speak to you are spirit, and they are life." (John 6:63) Therefore, the words of God are spirit and we cannot fully understand it except by the spirit, just as the Lord told the Samaritan woman: "God is Spirit, and those who worship Him must worship in spirit and truth." (John 4:24)

There are a lot of things in the Bible that we cannot understand with the mind alone, rather by the spirit. For example, when Mary, Martha's sister, sat at the feet of the Lord talking with Him, the Bible did not mention the conversation between the Lord Jesus and Mary but we can figure this out by spirit if we imagined ourselves sitting next to Mary at the feet of the Lord. The Lord promised that the Spirit will teach us everything and remind us of everything. (John 14:26) St Paul said: "It is written: "Eye has not seen, nor ear heard, Nor have entered into the heart of man the things which God has prepared for those who love Him. But God has revealed them to us through His Spirit. For the Spirit searches all things, yes, the deep things of God." (1 Cor 2:9-11)

WITH REVERENCE:

We should always approach God with reverence, not that of a slave to his master but that of a son to his father. As we grow in our spiritual life and in our relationship with God, we shall increase in reverence towards Him and to His words. Certainly we did not reach David's spiritual level who said: "My heart stands in awe of Your word." (Psalm 119:161)

When we read or listen to the word of God, we should be in awe and reverence, as there is a difference between the words of God compared to that of man. St Paul teaches the believers of Thessalonica how to receive the Word of God by saying: "When you received the word of God which you heard from us, you welcomed it not as the word of men, but as it is in truth, the word of God, which also effectively works in you who believe." (1 Thes 2:13)

Let us feel that we are in the presence of God when we read the Bible. Some people, as a sign of respect to the Word of God, will only read the Bible standing. Others read it while kneeling down. The Holy Bible is a message from the heavenly Father to each one of His sons. We do not act as sons if we have a lack of respect to the Word. The Lord said through Malachi: "A son honors his father, and a servant his master. If then I am the Father, Where is My honor? And if I am a Master, Where is My reverence?" (Mal 1:6) Beware of not respecting the Word of God when you are studying it. Do not read it while lying in bed or in an improper position as if you are reading a newspaper or a magazine, unless you are obliged due to an illness for example. Our Lord loves us as His children but we should be respectful, and there is a special blessing for those who learn the Word of God in reverence. God said, through Isaiah the Prophet: "On this one will I look: On him who is poor and of a contrite spirit, And who trembles at My word." (Is 66:2)

What is said about reading is also about listening to the Word of God, for when the Lord speaks, heaven listens. Thus, when the deacon is about to read the Gospel in church, he warns the congregation saying: "Stand up in the fear of God and listen to the Holy Gospel," then he announces that he is approaching the Word of God saying "Blessed is he who comes in the name of our Lord God Saviour and King of us all Jesus Christ the Son of the Living

God, glory be to Him forever Amen."

When Ezra the Scribe read the Book of the Law, "The ears of all the people were attentive to the Book of the Law" and when he opened it, all the people stood up. They bowed their heads and worshiped the LORD, with their faces to the ground. All the people wept, when they heard the words of the Law. So the Levites silenced the people, saying, "Be still, for the day is holy; do not be grieved." (Neh 8:11) If that was the case during the time of the Law and the animal sacrifices, then how should we receive the Word of our Saviour, other than with awe and reverence?

WITH HUMBLENESS:

As we learn the Word of God in spirit and with reverence, we also study it with humbleness. The Lord will reveal His secrets to the humble: "You have hidden these things from the wise and prudent and have revealed them to babes." (Matt 11:25) Thus, he hides his secrets from those who think themselves wise, and reveals his secrets to those who are humble.

As we endeavour to read the Word of God, let us prepare our minds, leave any worldly engagement, cross ourselves with the Holy Cross and pray that the Lord may bless this time. We also should declare our ignorance and shortcomings and no doubt God will respond. James, the apostle says "Receive with meekness the implanted word, which is able to save your souls." (James 1:21) Let us not depend solely on our mind to understand, for this has led to the fall of many and resulted in heresy. If we find difficulty in understanding, we should consult recognised books that explain the Bible, those which were written by well known writers, who believed in the correct doctrine. St Peter wrote about the Epistles of St Paul: "Speaking in them of these things, in which are some things hard to understand, which untaught and unstable people twist to their own destruction, as they do also the rest of the Scriptures." (2 Peter 3:16) Thus, it is important to read reliable interpretations of the Holy Bible.

Sadly, many people have decided to explain the Holy Bible according to their own understanding without consulting the fathers of the early church and the saints. This has led to many heresies and divisions in the church, and the world has now become deprived from the blessing of having one church.

WITH THE GUIDANCE OF THE HOLY SPIRIT:

No one can explain the meaning of a book better than the author. No one can clarify the verses in a poem more than the poet. This analogy can be applied to the Holy Bible. If you want to understand the Holy Bible, ask for the guidance of the Holy Spirit that inspired the saints to write it. The Lord Jesus promised that the Holy Spirit will teach us everything and remind us of all that He said. (John 14:26) "For the Spirit searches all things, yes, the deep things of God." (1 Cor 2:10) Talk to Him in your heart and tell Him: "Open my eyes, that I may see wondrous things from Your law." (Psalm 119:18)

A simple believer, who depends on God and the help of the Holy Spirit, can understand a lot from the Holy Bible, better than a wise or educated person. St John said rightfully: "You do not need that anyone teach you; but as the same anointing teaches you concerning all things." (1 John 2:27) The anointing here means the anointing of the Holy Spirit, that which we receive in the Holy Sacrament of El Myroun. Please do not understand the part "You do not need that anyone teach you" as to depend totally on your mind. We have talked in the previous point about learning the Holy Bible with humbleness and that means not relying on our understanding and knowledge, "And lean not on your own understanding." (Prov 3:5)

It was said about St John Chrysostom, the Patriarch of Constantinople, that a young man came to church to ask him about a certain matter and the Patriarch asked him to come later to the office. The young man came to the office a couple of times, but every time the Patriarch's disciple turned him down saying that St John was busy. One day the Patriarch asked his disciple about the young man and if he came to see him. The disciple replied that whenever the young man came, he saw that the Patriarch was busy writing and that there was a man sitting next to him dictating. At that time St John was writing his book about the meaning of the Epistles of St Paul. When the Patriarch asked who that man was, the disciple said he did not see him before but he looked like a picture hanging in the office. St John knew then that St Paul himself came to assist him in the interpretation of his Epistles!

FOR PERSONAL BENEFIT:

To be able to enjoy the Holy Bible, we must study it for our own personal benefit. If you are a servant, do not study it just to get a useful subject to teach your class but your main aim is to benefit yourself and be satisfied. Then you can benefit others and fulfil them. It is important to sit with the Holy Bible for a sustained period of time, not just minutes, in order to be fulfilled from the living Bread.

When reading the Holy Bible, try to find a personal message from God. It is good to stop every now and then and ask yourself "What does the Lord want from me as I read this passage?" Learn from Samuel, who when he was in the temple said: "Speak, LORD, for Your servant hears." (1 Sam 3:10) Let us listen attentively to the Word of God in order to comprehend its meaning.

You should feel that the Holy Bible is a personal message from your heavenly Father. Do not take it as a general message to mankind. For there is a difference when a believer feels that Jesus suffered and died for him personally, than that He died for the salvation of the world. This is clear in St Paul's life. We hear him saying: "The Son of God, who loved me and gave Himself for me" (Gal 2:20); "In the day when God will judge the secrets of men by Jesus Christ, according to my gospel." (Rom 2:16) Similarly, there is a difference between a person who reads news from a newspaper and one who reads the same news from a letter from his own father. The message of the Holy Bible is a personal message to each one of us.

Try to benefit from what you read; If you read about His mercy towards the sinners, raise your heart and pray that the Lord may be merciful to you also. When you read about Jesus visiting a house, pray diligently that He may come and visit your house. When you read that Jesus opened the eyes of a blind person, pray that He may open your eyes too, and so on. The Lord wants us to ask, for

He said: "Until now you have asked nothing in My name. Ask, and you will receive, that your joy may be full." (John 16:24)

Study the Book regularly and do not think that there are some useful chapters while others are difficult for "All Scripture is given by inspiration of God, and is profitable for doctrine, for reproof, for correction, for instruction in righteousness, that the man of God may be complete, thoroughly equipped for every good work." (2 Tim 3:16, 17) Specify a certain amount of time for reading every day and increase it whenever you can.

To benefit more from your reading, make a point to study the Word. Assign a copybook and write your own comments, compare passages and points from different parts of the Bible, "Comparing spiritual things with spiritual." (1 Cor 2: 13) It is also good to underline some of the verses. Do not just read the Holy Book for blessing but study the Word and be satisfied spiritually.

WAYS TO STUDY THE HOLY BIBLE

There is no specific way to study the Holy Bible but each one should be comfortable in a way that suits him. Here we present some approaches:

1- The most used way is following the spiritual principles which we discussed earlier. That is to pray at the beginning and at the end, to study the Word in reverence and humbleness, to memorise verses and compare passages. Summarise each chapter, learn new verses and end each period by prayer. It is commendable that as we study a chapter, we recall the previous three chapters. This method suits personal study, family or small groups.

2- Some people use books of interpretation as they study the Holy Bible. They write comments on each chapter and may keep a notebook with their chosen verses, comments and questions. Some re-bind the Holy Bible with plain paper so they can write some notes.

3- In addition to the above, some try to apply what they have studied. They would study a passage in the morning and choose a point or verse to try and follow during the day. At the end of the day, they will review their behaviour to check if they applied what they studied. They will pray to the Lord to help them in their efforts.

Others would prefer to take a certain exercise to follow for the whole week, rather than only for a day. As they study the Holy Bible, they write any other exercises to follow later.

4- Others will link their study with prayer, dedicating certain times. This is the correct way to study the Book. They will pray first then study a passage and contemplate in it for a while to learn what is of benefit to their lives. Afterwards, they pray again that the Lord may keep what they learned in their hearts. Some youth use this method to study the Holy Bible individually, then they meet together to discuss in spiritual groups.

5- Another method is to study the Holy Bible by topic. They have a special notebook divided into topics such as: prayer, purity, love, faith, service, and so on. As one studies the Holy Bible, he will look for verses that relate to each topic and write them in his notebook. When he finishes studying the whole Holy Bible, he would have gathered many verses for each topic.

6- There is also group Bible study where a certain passage is chosen for everyone to study separately, and then they gather to hear each other's comments and answer any questions.

Another way for a group Bible study is to read a passage aloud and get all those present to give their opinions or questions, with the leader commenting at the end. Some fear that this way may result in faulty interpretations, while others think it is good to express different views so that corrections can be made. It is important, in group Bible study that each one participates in a humble way, not as a wise person educating the others. Everyone should be aware of the presence of God. It is also important that the leader is a spiritual person who has studied the Holy Bible properly, and is aware of other teachings as well.

THE COPTIC CHURCH AND THE HOLY BIBLE

The Coptic Church pays much attention to the Holy Bible. This is apparent in all its services. It presents to the congregation a living model of how important the Holy Bible is. It teaches its children to pray the prayers of the hours (Agpia) daily. The prayers of the hours consist of some Psalms that suit each hour, as well as a passage from the Holy Bible. It is known that the Psalms are full of prophecies about our Lord Almighty.

The praises that are sung prior to the evening and morning vespers, and the Holy Liturgy, are passages from the Holy Bible.

The Holy Liturgy's prayers are all taken from different parts of the Holy Bible. In addition, there are readings from different Books of the Bible like the Epistles of St Paul, Acts and the Gospel. Before reading the Bible, the priest prays the Words of Jesus Christ: "O Lord Jesus Christ who said to his holy disciples and pure apostles blessed are your eyes for they see, and your ears for they hear; for assuredly, I say to you that many prophets and righteous men desired to see what you see, and did not see it, and to hear what you hear, and did not hear it." (Matt 13:16,17) After that, the priest gives his sermon according to the Gospel of the day.

Throughout the whole year, the church chooses certain readings which are appropriate for the occasion, so that its children may remember them. For example, the readings of Passion Week are read before the Resurrection; this week is full of various readings from different passages of the Holy Bible as it includes the last week in the life of Jesus Christ on earth. On Holy Friday, all readings concentrate on the suffering of our Lord, reminding us of His crucifixion. The church stays vigil all night until early Saturday, praying various praises from the Old Testament and reading the Book of Revelation.

If we look into all the prayers that the church uses in any occasion, whether baptism, wedding, or funeral, we find it is all taken directly from the Holy Bible.

Our Coptic Church encourages its children to study the Word of God as daily spiritual nourishment. It is keen to teach its children to learn and follow the Holy Bible in all aspects of their lives.

Spiritual Exercises

✕

"This being so, I myself always strive to have a conscience without offense toward God and men."
(Acts 24:16)

- Spiritual Exercises: Benefits and Experience
- Sources of Spiritual Exercises
- Spiritual exercise and its Characteristics
- Duration of the Exercise
- Exceptions for an Exercise
- Reasons for an Exercise and its Encouragement
- Exercise notebook

SPIRITUAL EXERCISES: ITS BENEFITS AND EXPERIENCES

Spiritual readings – from any source – continue to be just reading material for mere intellectual knowledge, until it becomes exercises that are part of your life. For whatever you practice, will become a habit by time and will be easier to perform. Similarly, what is easy to perform will eventually be part of your nature and one of your characteristics. This is a benefit of spiritual exercises.

A person who practices spiritual exercises will gradually gain virtues. He will acquire a more pure heart day after day and experience the spiritual life. When he talks to people about spiritual exercises, he is talking from personal experience and not a theoretical one. He will not only acquire knowledge of the righteous path but also the difficulties that obstruct these paths and how to overcome each one.

He will also know himself, including his strong and weak characteristics. He will be able to recognize the difference between wanting to do good and the ability of doing it. He will acknowledge the warfare that he can face with the Grace of God and the situations from which he has to escape. With these exercises, a person will apprehend his spiritual status. He will see what the Lord has given him, so far as certain abilities and talents. As a result, he will not seek what is above him and he will know his limitations, so as not to go beyond it or boast about it. As a person recognises himself, he will be able to seek his confession father's advice more precisely as his confessions will become more clear and comprehensive. This will enable the priest to advise him properly.

A person who experiences spiritual exercises will not only understand the ways of the Lord and its signs and difficulties, he will understand himself, his strengths and weaknesses, and will have compassion for those who struggle. Through experience, he realises the temptations of the enemy and his wickedness; he recognises the times when a person is lukewarm and the times when the Grace of God departs for a while and the reasons behind it. Thus, those who succeeded in their spiritual exercises are the most compassionate towards those who struggle. They are able to endure the wrong doings of others and are able to support those in trouble. They do not judge those who fall, for they themselves had fallen, yet have risen again. At the same time, they know how easy one can fall and how difficult it is to rise again.

A person who has experienced spiritual exercises knows the different kinds of sins; the sins that fight the soul from the outside and those that fight from within. This person knows when the soul should respond to outward influences and when it should struggle strongly against it. He knows the situations where sin enters and steals the soul and he knows the situations that invite virtue. He can also recognise the diseases of the spirit, including the hidden ones.

SOURCES OF SPIRITUAL EXERCISES

Spiritual exercises are either negative or positive. The negative ones include training yourself to fight certain sins, or treating personal deficiencies or shortcomings. The positive ones are training yourself on certain virtues and spiritual characteristics. Therefore, the most important sources of spiritual exercises are:

(a) Previous Sins: I sit with myself and give a precise account to recognise my sins. You will find sins that happen less frequently than others, and ones that occur regularly. These sins should be included in your spiritual exercises so that you attempt to remove them. Know the reasons and sources for these sins. Be conscious of how it starts and take these first steps into your spiritual training to uproot these sins. Spiritual exercises can conquer both sinful habits and deficiencies.

(b) The Holy Bible: The word of God is the light for your life as it shows you the way to go. You can use verses and commandments to train yourself in performing what God demands of you, as presented by His Prophets and Apostles.

(c) The general practices of the church: This is very important and you should start with following the tradition and discipline of the church and its general worship process, as practiced by all believers. This is done not just because it is an order from the church but because the church and its service are directed by the Holy Spirit for the benefit of the believers' spiritual life. It is not proper that a person decides to train himself on certain practices in worshipping while neglecting church worship, which is a fellowship among all believers who are of one spirit. For example, it is not proper that a person imposes special fasting for himself while neglecting the general periods of fasting organised by the church. The same applies for spiritual meetings and prayers.

Examples for these general practices of the church include: Regular and early church attendance, studying and participating in hymns, studying rites, practicing general church prayers such as hourly prayers and annual praises, attending different occasions of the church, and abiding by the fasts organised by the church. You can also practise humility through these prayers and learn to listen carefully.

(d) General social virtues: Many people practice virtues of worship but neglect general social virtues which may result in mistakes not suitable for the servants of God. A person should train himself to be a loving member of his family, willing to serve them and willing to do the same in his surrounding society. In addition, he should train himself to treat others appropriately and become a successful member in society and at work.

(e) The biography of the saints: We can learn many virtues from the saints but a person needs to know his spiritual level so that he does not try, as a beginner, to practice what a saint reached after years of long-suffering. It is good to learn from the virtues of the saints and try to imitate them, but this has to be done wisely. That is, by choosing what is suitable for us and for our spiritual level, without expecting sudden change.

(f) Reasons for failure in a certain exercise: When you are training yourself to do something, you will sometimes feel that you cannot do this. Use this feeling of failure as a subject for a new exercise.

For example: You may have trained yourself not to judge others, yet you fail one day and judge people after participating in a discussion about the general policies of the church. Turn this into an exercise and train yourself not to enter into such discussions until you know how to express yourself without falling into judgement. At least, train yourself to be cautious when such subjects are discussed in front of you.

THE SPIRITUAL EXERCISE AND ITS CHARACTERISTICS

Many failed in their spiritual exercises because of the exercise itself. Thus, we will list some of the characteristics that should be present to help ensure the success of an exercise:

(a) Clarity of the exercise: For instance, do not train yourself on a virtue that is not too clear for you. Some have the following titles for their exercise: Meekness or Love of God, while they are not aware of the exact meaning of this exercise. Consequently, they become confused and fail. Therefore, it is important to clarify the exercise before yourself.

(b) Specify the exercise: Do not take "the mothers of virtues" or "total virtues" as a subject for your exercise, for this is too much for you. Rather, divide these virtues into branches, as separate exercises. For example, do not take the virtue of love as an exercise, for it is a general word and covers the whole Christian life. St Paul the Apostle mentioned some of its characteristics in his first Epistle to the Corinthians (13:4-7) where he mentioned 14 features. You cannot train yourself on all of them at the same time. The same applies to other virtues like meekness, humility, service, total prayer, silence or calmness. All these virtues are "total virtues" so take a small branch from these virtues and train yourself. A specific exercise is much easier to follow.

It is better not to train on too many exercises at the same time as some people choose to train on five or six items within the one go. This will decrease your concentration and your success of achievement.

People with a passionate heart and a spiritual jealousy, may object as this method is slow and will take a long time. They want to reach the end of the road quickly. Our advice to those is that the spiritual life needs long suffering and patience. It is not important for a person to reach a virtue quickly for then they may lose it quickly. The importance is to stick with a virtue, until it is maintained. Therefore, do not worry, my brother, and do not hesitate. Walk calmly in your spiritual way for a slow but steady step is much better than an unsteady step. The Lord may bless you with His Grace to motivate you. Do not let this push you into pride. Do not feel that you are almost complete. Only realise that it is a temporary visitation of Grace and you will return to your natural state. These visitations are not permanent and each person's life faces many changes.

(c) The occasion of the exercise: you need to choose the right exercise for the right occasion. For instance, do not practice silence on a day of celebration or on a day out with friends. Such an exercise will most probably fail. If you are worried about falling into gossip, do not put yourself under a total silence exercise but train yourself to avoid just gossip. These exercises may fail if they were not compatible to the social standard, suitable time, family circumstances, condition of society, educational level or special spiritual level.

(d) Gradual training: High jumps in spiritual life are not safe, especially after a sudden fall or retraction. Those who take large jumps at once may succeed initially because of their enthusiasm, but they will not continue for a long time.

Thus, it is important to follow exercises gradually, walking step by step. Every step you walk forward, stabilise your foot quickly before taking another step. Therefore, if you are faced with a problem and have to take a backward step, you will be a able to go further than before after resting a bit on those previous stable steps. However, if you jump quickly, you will not find a place to rest or stabilise yourself.

An example:

Two people trained themselves on silence. The first practised silence in one immediate step. However, the other trained himself gradually, by first avoiding judgement, then reducing useless talk and then avoiding talking in subjects that were not suitable for him. With time, the second person got used to short replies, not interrupting others, talking in a calm and low voice, not gossiping, not talking unnecessarily, and keeping quiet when there were discussions that he did not know enough about. Consequently, if these two people needed to talk, the second, who practiced silence gradually, started talking slowly and cautiously, while the first one returned to his original state, in judging and hurting others. The first would have talked in many useless subjects, he would have fallen into many mistakes and would have had to start from the beginning again.

DURATIONS OF AN EXERCISE

The history of the saints gives us some insight into the duration of a spiritual exercise. Some saints took a year to practise one exercise. However, this is not long as St Agathson learnt silence over three years.

Some may ask "How can I train myself on many virtues if each one will take such a long time?" The answer is clear, for virtues are linked to each other and lead to each other.

For example, if a person has excelled in constant prayer and keeps on praying as often as he can, he must have kept silent for long periods. In turn, silence will necessitate seclusion. He will not socialise with many people and consequently avoid the necessity to speak. As he spends long periods praying, he would not be eating much, thus helping him fast. The nature of prayer leads itself to fasting, and fasting leads itself to silence, silence leads to meditation, and meditation will provide a chance for reading and studying the Holy Bible. All this will lead to an effort to purify his heart and his thoughts. Prayer assists in purity. The mind that is busy with the Lord will not leave a chance to the devil. Fasting also assists in purity as it strains the body and its lusts. Thus, here we see that a person was training himself, theoretically on one virtue, while practically he trained himself on many linked virtues.

A short period is not enough to benefit from an exercise and that is why Mar Isaac says: "Any exercise that is practiced for a short period of time will have no fruits." On the contrary, if it is practiced for a longer time, it will be of great benefit. St Isaac says: "Know my son, every exercise according to its length and training, will be of benefit."

So if these great saints lengthened their training for years, then what about a normal believer? So give yourself enough time in each exercise and do not leave it until you reach satisfactory results. Try to resist boredom and monotony that may attack during your training. A person who jumps from one exercise to another quickly will not give himself a chance to benefit from either.

As a medium solution: you may take a large and main exercise that can extend for a long period of time while taking beside it a smaller exercise that can be finished in couple of weeks or more.

EXCEPTIONS FOR AN EXERCISE

There are some exercises that have no exceptions, which are those which fight against sin. A person, who is training himself to resist a sin of impurity, cannot have exceptions that allow him to do such sins. However, there are exceptions when dealing with virtues such as fasting, praying, silence, seclusion exercises and others dealing with meekness and humility.

A certain exercise should not tie or chain a person down. An exercise is set for a person and not the person for the exercise.

For example, a person may fall into many mistakes every time he talks. As a result, he may practice silence as St Arsanious says, "I spoke many times and I regretted it each time, while I never regretted remaining silent." Such a person cannot be a slave to silence especially if he lives in the world and the social life demands his talking. Actually, there are certain situations when it is a sin against the Lord and against people when one does not speak. In such cases, one must speak and consider these as exceptions from his exercise. In other situations, the benefit of speaking is much more than that of silence. St Barsinophios says, "Speaking for the sake of the Lord is good, and silence for the sake of the Lord is good." King Solomon says, "To everything there is a season...a time to keep silence, and a time to speak." (Ecc 3:1, 7) By these exceptions, a person will know when to speak and when to be silent; on what subjects to speak and on what to keep be silent; with whom to speak and with whom to keep quiet. By these exceptions, a person will learn when to speak in detail and when to speak briefly; when to be soft and pleasant in speech, and when to be firm and serious. A person who knows all of the above has learned the exercise of silence, and such a person can speak anytime for he knows his limitations. However, he who offends another with his silence or makes another angry by his silence is like a Pharisee who lives by the letter and not by the spirit

REASONS FOR AN EXERCISE AND ITS BENEFITS

A person is encouraged to keep an exercise, overcome its difficulties and understand the wisdom behind it. The benefits of an exercise are numerous, especially if it is extracted from the Holy Bible, the saying of the fathers or the biography of saints.

When a person starts an exercise too quickly, without knowing its benefits, the exercise may not succeed. When this person faces an obstacle, he will question the benefits of the exercise and leave it immediately.

So, before starting an exercise, sit with yourself, understand it and be convinced of it. Take advice, for the exercise may or may not be beneficial for you, depending on your circumstances. When you are sure of its personal benefit, learn a verse or two that may encourage you, especially when you face an obstacle. Try to remember the sayings of the fathers and the stories of the saints in relation to this subject. All this will help you renew your energy and give you the strength to perform it. Always remind yourself of your exercise, so as not to forget it.

Pray long prayers for the success of this exercise, and do not think that by your strength or will power you will succeed without any difficulty! For you do not know the enemy's attacks and you may not know your personal weakness. Ask the help of the Lord and know that without Him you can do nothing. Consequently, when you succeed, thank God for His support and do not imagine that it was from your personal strength.

EXERCISE NOTEBOOK

This is a necessary tool in reminding and encouraging you of your exercises. It also helps in checking and keeping account of your performance. Let this notebook be a complete record and use it to write all necessary information.

Write the title of the exercise and its benefits briefly. Include verses, sayings of the fathers, and the duration and date of the exercise. You will then write the dates of the days on the side of the page and leave a couple of lines for each day as you see fit. Record your comments on these lines as you assess yourself at the end of every day.

If the exercise was a complete success, then you may write "Thank you God", or you may add some of the reasons that helped you to perform it. You may also write "Nothing happened to examine the success of this exercise." If you break the exercise, you may record the number of times you broke it, when and with whom. Did you break the whole exercise or part of it? Where there necessary reasons for breaking the exercise or was it broken out of your own choice? All these notes will assist in avoiding future failure and can be used as material for the exercise. You may also record exceptions to the exercise. Some people encourage themselves by grading their progress daily.

It is advisable to gather and summarise this information at the end of the week. Derive facts that can be of benefit for you later.

Others may write additional information in their exercise notebook, such as someone starting their notebook with the following prayer:

"Without you Lord, I can do nothing. My soul is wandering and I cannot get hold of it. These exercises are a kind of prayer where I declare my desire to live with You. I do not want to depend on human ability, so please facilitate my way with your Grace."

EXAMPLES OF SOME EXERCISES

1. GENTLENESS EXERCISES

- Do not anger, upset or annoy anyone.

- Do not be upset from anyone.

- Be calm in everything (calm in speaking, walking and working. Have an inward calmness and do not let anything trouble you.)

- Use a low voice.

- Do not speak as one with authority. (Do not shout or scold.)

- Treat elders and youth with respect. (Give many compliments.)

- Do not interfere in others' business. (Do not impose your personality on others, through pressure, criticism, or rebuke.)

- Do not contradict a dialogue (Do not object other people's opinions but listen to them.)

- Do not interrupt a dialogue, even if you heard the conversation many times previously. Be an active listener.

- Do not complain, and if you do, direct it at a situation, not at a person.

- Tolerate the faults of others by longsuffering

- Be pleasant with everyone

- Be gentle

- Be obedient and submissive. (This includes submitting to the advice of your confession father.)

2. EXERCISES ON JUDGEMENT

- Avoid analysing people, (Do not talk about other people's jobs and characteristics. Do not gossip.)

- Avoid cursing

- Avoid complaining about people (if necessary, mention only the specific point and not the name of the person)

- Avoid showing disgust (either by movement, sign, or in silence – for it is a kind of judgement, even though you are not talking.)

- Avoid judging a group

- Avoid indirect judgement (When you speak indirectly about people, others may judge according to what they understood from your words.)

- Avoid talking about certain politics (This usually ends up with judgement.)

- Avoid talking about people whom you do not have a clear conscious about

- Do not defend yourself by blaming others

- Resist and dismiss any thought of judgement.

3. EXERCISES FOR SILENCE

There are exercises written within the chapter on "Silence." Some gentleness and judgement exercises will also apply with silence.

4. PRAYER EXERCISES

- Make your body modest. (This includes, raising the hands, standing upright, bowing and preserving the senses.) These exercises can be practiced one at a time.

- Keep your heart modest, by feeling the presence of the Lord.

- Pray with the Agpia. This helps you increase the quantity and quality of your prayers.

- Memorise Psalms and parts, so you can pray during times when you have no access to an Agbia.

- Pray your Personal prayers, in addition to the Psalms

- Pray the Jesus Prayer (My Lord Jesus Christ have mercy on me) or any similar prayer.

- Practice constant prayer (while walking, during work or while travelling.)

- Start any work with prayer (For example, pray before eating, before reading, before studying and before serving.)

- Extend your prayer times. For example, pray before sleeping, to preserve yourself from bad dreams. Pray before eating, to preserve yourself from the lust of the flesh. This process can be gradual and you may add memorised prayers to it.

- Do not pray for requests only. Do not pray for the sake of asking for God's help. Pray out of your love for God. Thank God, praise God and confess before him, before making petitions.

- Pray for enemies and for those who hurt you.

5. FASTING EXERCISES

(This needs special wisdom so that one's work and responsibilities are not affected.)

- Fast according to Church Rites

  (For example, Wednesdays, Fridays, Holy Forty days, Passion Week, etc.)

- Conduct Special Fasts for certain situations, for oneself or for others.

- Manage the Period of your fasting. It differs from one person to another. A person should start gradually. For example, do not eat or drink immediately after waking up.

- Monitor the kinds of food you eat. It is not only about eating fasting food. There may be fasting foods that you love and long to eat. Fasting foods should not be eaten with pleasure.

- Monitor the quantity of your food. Fasting is not just about eating fasting food, but eating in small quantities.

- Monitor the quantity of your drink. Drinking should also be specified, like food. The quantity will depend on the season and occasion and should be monitored in a wise way.

- Do not eat between meals

- Leave out additional food, like some drinks and sweets.

- Do not show off that you are fasting, even if you have to leave out an exercise and compensate for it another time.

- Give offerings from what is saved from fasting. For example, if a person skips a meal, he can give its cost to the poor in addition to ordinary offerings.

Note: Some fasts have certain orders and restrictions, such as Passion Week. The church requests fasting until sunset and breakfast should be with bread and salt. If you cannot do that then avoid sweet foods or foods most enjoyable for you. Fast for as long as you are physically capable.

Solitude

꧑

"It is good for a man to bear the yoke in his youth.
Let him sit alone and keep silent."
(Lam 3:27-28)

INTRODUCTION

Why do I often sin and stray away from God? Why do I deviate spiritually? Why am I facing many problems and am unable to solve them? The reason is in one thing: I do not know myself properly.

So where can I see myself clearly without any pretence? Where can I know the truth as the Lord said: "You will know the Truth and the Truth will set you free." Where can I see the Lord?

Can I see myself in this busy life? Can I see the Lord among many people? No. I will not know myself unless I am alone in the presence of God. There, I can have a close look at my behaviour. I will not see God in His glory except on the Mount of Transfiguration, that is, when I leave the world behind, even for a while, and go up to the mountain of contemplation.

+ + +

Since creation, Mankind was not affected by the rapidness of life, compared with nowadays. There are many distractions in our world. Our era is a speedy era where life is too quick and everyone is trying to cope. Woe to those who are attached to it and woe to those who are left behind!

Many wrong ideas and trends creep into our society and into our spiritual life as well. We are not aware of it as we are too busy coping with all the changes in life.

These trends are not only in the world at large but also in the service. Many blessed people who were quite active in their service became too tired and were lost!

It is a shame that some servants are very busy and feel they are doing what the Lord wants. Be careful lest you hear at the end: "Go away I do not know you."

Many servants lack grace. They think that their service and activity is satisfactory while they are deceiving themselves. The important thing is to: "Put on the Lord Jesus Christ, and make no provision for the flesh, to fulfill its lusts." (Rom 13:14)

BLESSINGS OF SOLITUDE

We all need solitude. We all need to examine our behaviour and fix what the world spoiled.

If you really want to know yourself and your spiritual fruits, (for you are a branch in the real Vine, our Lord Jesus Christ), go into your room, close your door, sit calmly and look within yourself. You will then see your poverty, need, nakedness and shame. You will realize that "you are wretched, miserable, poor, blind, and naked." (Rev 3:17)

You will see that the branch of your life has no fruit and you know that every tree that does not bear fruit is cut down and thrown in fire.

You will clearly see your sins. You will realize your hypocrisy, even if it is unintentional. You will fear the apostle's words "My brethren, let not many of you become teachers, knowing that we shall receive a stricter judgment." (James 3:1)

You will see your picture in God's mirror and discover your ugliness. You are not like Him though you were created in His image and likeness. You were invited to be the image of His Son who was a firstborn among many brethren. (Rom 8:29)

It is a great blessing that a person discovers his sins gets rid of them. One of the saintly fathers say: "A person's knowledge of himself is a sure method to know God."

What is the use of knowing myself when I sit on my own? I will know my sin and weakness, "For I know that in me (that is, in my flesh) nothing good dwells." (Rom 7:18) What is the advantage of knowing my weakness? When I know my weakness, I know God "for My strength is made perfect in weakness." (2 Cor 12:9) "For when I am weak, then I am strong." (2 Cor 12:10) When I feel the bitterness of my sin, I will then deserve grace.

St Peter said to the Lord: "Leave my boat Lord, for I am a sinful man." St Peter felt his sinful condition and so the Lord replied, "Do not be afraid, from now you will catch men." St Peter deserved this high status of discipleship and service when he realized who he really was and confessed, "I am a sinful man." Therefore, by knowing ourselves, we will know God. However, we cannot achieve this in the crowd and noise of the world, but in solitude and quietness.

In solitude, you have the chance to plead with God, feel sorry and weep. You do not have this chance amidst the noise of the world.

The practice of solitude and contemplation is a successful way to train and develop one's personality. Solitude is a school for virtues, a ladder leading upwards and the shortest way to God, as we directly listen to the Holy Spirit. You cannot hear the tender tune of a violin when the drums are beating or the horns blowing. Similarly, we cannot hear the voice of God in the crowd and noise of the world.

The woman, who was bleeding for a long time and spent all her money on physicians, secretly touched the hem of Jesus' garment and was cured on the spot. (Matt

9:20-23) Similarly, a tortured soul needs to sit with the Saviour, in a holy solitude, to be cured.

You cannot find true comfort while being attached to people and involving yourself in everyday's obligations, for the Lord said, "When you pray, go into your room, and when you have shut your door, pray to your Father who is in the secret place." (Matt 6:6)

Solitude gives rest to your tired soul, tears to wash your dirt, and a spirit that can cry out saying, "I forget to eat my bread because of the sound of my groaning, my bones cling to my skin." (Psalm 102:4-5) If you want a pure heart that God describes as a heart after His own heart (Acts 13:22), then follow David the Prophet who says, "Indeed, I would wander far off, and remain in the wilderness." (Psalm 55:7) Do this in your life by practicing periods of solitude.

JOHN THE BAPTIST:

Though he was very holy and deserved the Lord's testimony, he escaped to the wilderness from an early age until he emerged to Israel. He chose to escape from the world though he became holy by the Holy Spirit, while in his mother's womb.

JOHN THE BELOVED:

He did not deserve to witness the Revelation, which he recorded for the whole world except during his time alone on Patmos Island. He was "in the spirit." (Rev 1:10)

ST PAUL THE GREAT:

After the Lord revealed Himself while he was on his way to Damascus, St Paul went to Arabia (a desert east of Damascus). He said about himself: "I did not immediately confer with flesh and blood, nor did I go up to Jerusalem to those who were apostles before me; but I went to Arabia." (Gal 1:16-17) In this wilderness, he enjoyed a holy solitude with the Lord where he received all the instructions needed for his life and the growth of the holy church. This period was about three years.

He later said, "For I received from the Lord that which I also delivered to you." (1 Cor 11:23) So how did St Paul receive these matters if he was not one of the disciples and did not meet Jesus on earth? It was through his holy solitude with the Lord in Arabia.

Isaiah the Prophet was fed heavenly bread when he was alone. However, while among people, he hardly found anything to eat. The children of Israel ate manna only in the deserted wilderness. Similarly, only the soul that lives in solitude will gain the blessings of it.

What did Abraham do to become a great nation? He obeyed God by leaving his country, his family and his father's house. Therefore, you too, get out of your country, leave your family and your father's house and depart to a holy solitude so that the Lord may bless you and make you a great nation. (Gen 12:1-2)

Many saints loved solitude and lived it. St Arsanius, the teacher of Kings' children, is a clear example for those who lived that way. When he escaped from Constantinople and lived in El Eskeet, he spent three years praying and pleading to the Lord to guide him as to what to do and how to act.

Finally, he heard a voice saying: "Arsanius, be calm, stay away from people and be silent; For by doing these things you may avoid sin and be saved." When he heard this voice again, he escaped from all brethren and forced himself to stay calm and silent. At one point, Pope Thawphilus the 23rd wanted to see him so he sent messengers to his cell. St Arsanius replied: "If you come, I will open the door for you; if I open for you, I will not be able to close it in front of others; and if I open for all people then I will not be able to live here." He loved solitude so much that during the Holy Liturgy, he used to pray behind a pillar, at the back of the church. No one used to see him and he used to see no one. This pillar still exists in el Baramos Monastery.

St Anthony the Great says: "If your mind remains away from people and becomes quiet, God will strengthen it and enable it to ask and search for what is Godly; to be ready to witness the greatness and Divinity of the Lord."

Is there any better proof about the blessings of solitude, than that the Lord Himself loved it "Now when it was day, He departed and went into a deserted place. And the crowd sought Him and came to Him, and tried to keep Him from leaving them." (Luke 4:42) You too go to the wilderness and meet the Lord Jesus. Sit at His feet in a holy solitude as Mary (Martha's sister) did. "Mary has chosen that good part, which will not be taken away from her." (Luke 10:42)

We receive many blessings when we sit with God. At the beginning, the soul will hear, "The Teacher has come and is calling for you." (John 11:28) At the end of solitude, the soul will say, "It is good to be here." As the feeling of love increases, the soul will see nothing but the Lord Jesus Christ himself. (Matt 17:1-8)

WHAT IS SOLITUDE?

Staying away from people is not solitude for a person may be sitting alone but the world is living in his heart. We cannot say this person is in solitude! Solitude is to empty the heart and mind from all worldly affairs.

Real solitude is to be alone with God: The mind is to be free from any worries, and the heart is to be empty of all desires, except the holy love towards the Beloved. Solitude should be in an isolated place, away from people and in an area where you can hear the silence! When the soul is ready, it can say, "Amen. Even so, come, Lord Jesus." (Rev 22:20) In response, the soul will hear, "The Teacher has come and is calling for you." (John 11:28)

The Lord Jesus spent time alone with His Father, "And everyone went to his own house. But Jesus went to the Mount of Olives." (John 7:53, 8:1) He used to spend the whole night in prayer. When the disciples were leaving, each to his own family, the Lord Jesus said confidently, "And yet I am not alone, because the Father is with Me." (John 16:32) Thus the Lord set an example of solitude for us, that is, being alone with the Father. Let us learn how to leave the world with its noise and problems, to enjoy solitude with the Lord and sing: "My beloved is mine, and I am his. He feeds his flock among the lilies." (Song of Songs 2:16)

Some people may object the idea of solitude, according to what the Apostle says, "Love does not seek its own." (1

Cor 13:5) However, we reply, "As for me, I will stick to the Lord, depend on Him and praise Him because this is Best." It is solitude for the heart, a quietness of heart. In spite of all his obligations with the kingdom, King David practised this as he often says, "I have set the LORD always before me." (Psalm 16:8)

THE SERVANTS' NEED FOR SOLITUDE

How poor are the servants these days! They lose their lives and their peace within their service! They are tired because they do not dedicate time to spend alone with the Lord. One of the fathers say: "Whoever dedicates his life to be a living sacrifice, must not throw himself totally in service but must also extend himself to solitude." A servant needs more spiritual effort than any other and must rely on the assistance of the Lord. If we acknowledge the importance of solitude in our lives, we will realize how much more important it is in the lives of servants.

A servant who leads others, must be filled with the Holy Spirit and must be able to correct his behaviour according to the Lord. Mar Isaac says, "The day that you do not spend in solitude, thinking about your mistakes, do not count that day as part of your life. Love solitude because it is where you can find yourself. Without solitude, you will only see others and will neglect seeing yourself."

HOW TO SPEND SOLITUDE

The only thing you do in solitude is Nothing. You just contemplate on yourself and discover the sins that are preventing you from enjoying the presence of God in your life. Do not spend your solitude time in preparing materials for your service or in thinking about the problems of the service. You want to spend this time in peace with yourself, praising the Lord, praying lovingly and longing for Him. You also review your life and your behaviour.

Leave behind all the interests of the world. It is good to spend this time especially while fasting and under the guidance of your confession father.

At first, you may be annoyed but force yourself to be patient so you can reap the fruits of solitude. Remember, my brother, solitude is not just spare time, after which you return to your previous life. It is an opportunity for repentance, a renewal of promises to the Lord, and for practicing any necessary spiritual exercises.

WHERE TO SPEND SOLITUDE

As individuals, we need to choose a certain place that is suitable for each of us. Preferably, use one location all the time so that you get used to it and are not distracted during your solitude time.

It is also necessary to have a house for solitude in every big city. This house will enable servants to enjoy a period of quietness. It should be in a quiet area, not too far from the city. It should be run by spiritual leaders and have a set of rules.

Spiritual Readings

✎

- ❧ Subject of these readings
- ❧ Purpose of reading
- ❧ Benefits of Spiritual Readings
- ❧ How to read
- ❧ Time and Duration of Reading

SUBJECT OF THESE READINGS

There are many different types of religious readings but here we will specify spiritual reading, i.e. readings that surround the spirit with the love of God, purifying the soul and body.

There are three main sources of spiritual readings:

- The Holy Bible - together with explanatory books, meditations, sermons and books about the saints in the Bible.

- The sayings of the fathers, monastic books and others about different virtues.

- Biographies of saints – monks, martyrs, servants, faithful heroes, leaders of Christian doctrines, etc...These books portray the highest standards of virtues and Christian values. Mar Isaac said: "The news of the saints is delightful to the humble listeners, just like drinking water to the young horses."

- Monitor the kinds of food you eat. It is not only about eating fasting food. There may be fasting foods that you love and long to eat. Fasting foods should not be eaten with pleasure.

PURPOSE OF READING

A person should read with an aim constantly in mind. For example, reading the Holy Bible can take different forms. Some people read the Bible to be familiar with its content, stories, commandments and personalities. Others read the Bible to gain spiritually by contemplating on certain verses and applying what they learn in their own lives.

However, there is also a third type of reading in which one studies the Holy Bible and attempts to understand its deeper meanings. It involves reading with great concentration and examining the stories more closely with the help of a dictionary and/or other older translations. It also involves studying the context of each book and comparing the different verses, symbols and prophesies. Such reading involves the study of difficult verses, even those that seem to contradict science, history, philosophy, etc...

All these types of readings are useful and necessary but here we want to discuss spiritual readings and meditations that are beneficial to the spirit and not merely the brain.

Benefits of Spiritual Readings

Reading requires concentration and so therefore our thoughts change according to the subjects of the materials we read. Mar Isaac says, "If mentioning virtuous people makes us think of imitating their virtue; then mentioning immoral people would make us think of imitating their sins. For remembering either of these people, our mind will think of their actions." Therefore, spiritual reading not only distracts our minds from material and worldly thoughts, but also lifts our minds to heavenly thoughts to taste the sweetness of the Lord.

Therefore, there is a passive and an active benefit of spiritual readings:

• The passive benefit is that spiritual readings prevent evil and useless thoughts from inhabiting the mind. Therefore, spiritual readings can sometimes be used as a weapon to cast out anger and relax the soul.

• The active benefit is that it raises the mind above all worldly cares to think of Godly matters. Gradually, spiritual readings can elevate one until he constantly thinks of God.

Spiritual reading is the door that leads the soul to spiritual warmth. A soul that becomes spiritually cold due to its engagement with material possessions, addiction to sin, busyness or evil thoughts, could gradually return to its warmth and strength through spiritual reading. This warmth, acquired from spiritual reading, can defeat whatever the soul is fighting against at the time, whether its boredom or laziness. It will also help the reader obtain virtues and resist worldly lusts.

A person will desire to imitate what he learns from the lives of saints and their virtues. As one continues in his spiritual readings, they will gradually start to apply what he learns and thus it becomes part of his life. Therefore, Pope Kyrillos VI once said, "Spiritual reading is a door to all virtues." Through spiritual reading, one can examine himself according to what he reads. Therefore, spiritual reading can become a tool to analyse one's standard and encourage them to repent.

As a one reads the biographies of the prophets, apostles and saints, they come to appreciate their high standards and the virtues that they have acquired through much hard work, dedication and patience. One can then be more aware of his own weaknesses and standards and therefore grow humble. Thus, spiritual readings can lead a person to clearly understand himself for the more he reads, the more he is humbled.

Spiritual reading is also a means of prayer. Prayer will be different according to the readings. Spiritual readings will help a person identify his sins and shortcomings so that he kneels in submission, confessing while asking for mercy and forgiveness. Another reading will simplify the virtues and its beauty, so a person will pray continuously asking God to help him obtain these virtues. Another type of spiritual reading will stress the importance of loving others and so a person will raise his hands praying on behalf of others. Another type of reading will describe God's superb qualities and eternal glory. This will in turn make one bow down and glorify God, feeling unworthy to even speak to God. Another reading will help one to feel the love of God so that he does not know what to say except words of praise and thanksgiving. Therefore, if spiritual reading is a motive for prayer, it is also means of prayer. Mar Isaac explained this saying that when one is about to pray, he remembers what he has read and can often use its words for praise.

Spiritual reading can also be used for contemplation. When one reads a verse or chapter in the Bible, they can often use their readings for meditation. Similarly, when one reads about one of the early desert fathers, they may use their readings to contemplate on God's Grace, the saint's love for God and their virtues. They can also store such spiritual thoughts in their mind for future reflection, for time spent in seclusion or in prayer. Such spiritual thoughts can never be acquired by those who read magazines and/ or exciting stories to merely satisfy their bodily desires.

Spiritual reading can also guide one along his path to God: It shows a person the Will of God and His Holy ways. David the Psalmist said "Your word is a lamp to my feet and a light to my path." (Psalm 119:105). A person reads the Word of God and the stories of the desert fathers, who were full of the Holy Spirit, gains insightful knowledge and wisdom which can help him to live a pure and proper life.

Spiritual reading is also beneficial in a variety of different situations. For example, a person may be troubled by a difficult problem and so when he reads, he finds something that supports him and shows him God's hand in a similar situation. Often these spiritual readings will also explain the behavior of early desert fathers who faced difficult problems, or they can explain the wisdom of God in allowing such trials. Such readings will lift his spirit and turn his sadness into joy. Another person might have sinned and might be struggling under the traps of the devil who is attempting to lead him into despair. Such a person may read something about salvation, repentance, God's mercy and acceptance. These readings in particular would give him hope and encourage him to repent and turn to God in prayer. Another example is of someone who has prayed a lot about a certain matter but feels that God is not listening to him because his prayers have not yet been answered. Such a person could read the Bible or a spiritual book about this subject and learn that God is always listening and will respond in due time.

Spiritual readings also helps keep the mind actively thinking of spiritual things and contemplating. Whoever reads a lot to contemplate will eventually be able to think in a spiritual way about anything he reads and benefit from it.

Finally, spiritual reading is a useful way to spend time and keep the mind engaged in useful thoughts. It assists in the life of seclusion and leaves no time for boredom or evil thoughts. It encurages the life of spiritual awarenes.

HOW TO READ

START READING WITH PRAYER:

Start your spiritual reading with prayer, asking the Holy Spirit to guide you and touch your heart. Explain to God your weaknesses and tell Him about your limited ability to understand. David the Psalmist said, "I have seen the consummation of all perfection, but Your commandment is exceedingly broad."(Psalm 119:96). Pray and ask God to open your mind to understand, your heart to accept what you have understood and the strength to carry out what you have accepted. Mar Isaac warns us saying: "Do not approach the secrets of the Holy Books without prayer and first asking for God's help." Therefore, prayer is clearly the key to understanding the truths in Holy Books.

TRY TO APPLY WHAT YOU HAVE LEARNT IN YOUR OWN LIFE:

Carry out whatever lessons you can do and what you cannot do, try to store it in your heart for later. Also, pray and ask for the intercession of the saints who were able to carry out those lessons that you cannot - this will keep you humble.

DURING MEDITATION, AVOID READING ABOUT PROBLEMS OR COMPLEX ISSUES:

Such complexities can be dealt with at later stages.

NOT ALL BOOKS OF THE **B**IBLE ARE SUITABLE FOR
MEDITATION FOR BEGINNERS - **S**TART WITH THE
HISTORICAL BOOKS FIRST:

First start reading about God's great characteristics and
His dealings with the saints. Read about the relationships
saints had with God and their dealings with others. Once
you have completed the historical books, it is recommended
that you read the educational books.

KNOW THAT READING IS A MEANS TO REACH AN
OBJECTIVE AND NOT AN OBJECTIVE IN ITSELF.

When you reach your goal, stop reading and
concentrate on your goal. Spend some time doing whatever
the Spirit guides you to do, whether it's meditation, prayer,
repentance or a spiritual exercise. This will inspire your
soul to love God more.

TIME AND DURATION OF
READING

A person needs spiritual reading for meditation as it is essential for the strengthening of the heart and mind. However, this kind of spiritual reading is not enough as it may only involve contemplating on a few verses. Years may pass and a person would still not have finished reading the Bible - it is important for a person to connect to different verses and obtain a deeper understanding of a certain topic.

Which type of spiritual reading should he choose? Is there a third type of reading which is for both studying and researching?

• Combine the two types of readings: A person may read a few chapters of the Holy Bible but only contemplate on a few verses or on a general idea. This method is most suitable for a busy person. Such a person should initially dedicate half an hour to God - twenty minutes spiritual reading and ten minutes contemplation - and then increase this time according to his ability.

• Distribute the different types of readings amongst the days of the week. A person can set a weekly schedule and may record a daily comment. This weekly schedule is more flexible and beneficial (as long as by the end of the week nothing is neglected).

• Spiritual reading accompanied by meditation should be set at a specific time for everyday of the week.

Reading merely for knowledge should be set for only a few days of the week, according to the time available.

• Use any spare time to read the Holy Bible and study it, without setting any restrictions on time or length of readings. This will provide you with the opportunity to retain other types of spiritual readings when the workload is too much.

In any case, make sure you choose an appropriate time for spiritual reading. If you read while you are tired, upset or busy, you will not enjoy the benefits of spiritual reading as much as you should and may even feel it a burder..

Service

ℵ

"The Son of Man did not come to be served, but to serve, and to give His life a ransom for many." (Matthew 20:28)

- What is service?
- Conditions of a good Servant
- Choosing and Preparation of a good servant
- Superficial service
- Strength in the life of a servant
- Spiritual leadership
- Refraining from the service
- All are invited to serve
- From Jerusalem to the end of the world

WHAT IS SERVICE?

Service is not an art which you can just gain through practice, nor a subject in which you can succeed by studying. It does not start in theological colleges, but rather in the heart - its college is that of the Holy Spirit which blazes, sanctifies and teaches the heart, reminding it of the sayings of the Lord Jesus Christ.

SERVICE IS HOLY LOVE

Service is holy love which fills the heart of a person who loves and lives for God, always tasting His sweetness "...taste and see that the Lord is good" (Psalm 34:8) Since service is holy love, it is unlimited with time or space. The aim of service is to show love to everybody, its message is for all mankind - not just for certain ranks of people.

SERVICE IS SPIRITUAL HAPPINESS

Service is an important source of human happiness. St Paul writes "And remember the words of the Lord Jesus, that He said, 'It is more blessed to give than to receive.'" (Acts 20:35) True happiness is not in keeping everything to ourselves, but rather in sharing whatever we have with others.

There are two types of lakes: fresh water and salt water lakes. Salt water lakes are often called 'closed lakes', as they only receive water but do not have any channels to give water. However, fresh water lakes continually give and take, thus making the water fresh.

Service fills the soul with happiness, as the Lord Jesus Christ rewards the righteous on Judgement Day saying, "...For I was hungry and you gave Me food; I was thirsty and you gave Me drink; I was a stranger and you took Me in; I was naked and you clothed Me; I was sick and you visited Me; I was in prison and you came to Me." (Matthew 25:35- 36)

How happy would a believer be when he feeds someone spiritual food and takes him to drink of the Living Water from which whoever drinks will never thirst? How happy would he be if he clothed a naked person with the robe of righteousness which he had previously lost... or if he presents a spiritually sick person to Jesus for healing, as seen by the four friends of the paralysed man...or if he visits a prisoner, bound by the chains of the devil, preaching to him about the Great Redeemer who can set him free of slavery as it is written "Jesus answered them, 'Most assuredly, I say to you, whoever commits sin is a slave of sin. And a slave does not abide in the house forever, but a son abides forever. Therefore if the Son makes you free, you shall be free indeed.'" (John 8:34-36)

The Lord Jesus said, "The Spirit of the Lord is upon Me, because He has anointed Me; to preach the gospel to the poor. He has sent Me to heal the broken-hearted, to proclaim liberty to the captives, and recovery of sight to the blind, to set at liberty those who are oppressed; to proclaim the acceptable year of the Lord." (Luke 4:18). How wonderful are Jesus words commenting on Isaiah the Prophet's statement, "Today this Scripture is fulfilled in your hearing." (Luke 4:21) This is service in its essence and blessings, and this is spiritual happiness in its origin and depth.

THE FIELD OF SERVICE

"....but the word of God is not chained." (2 Timothy 2:9) When St Paul and St John were instructed by the chief priests not to preach about Christ they replied saying, "Whether it is right in the sight of God to listen to you more than to God, you judge. For we cannot but speak the things which we have seen and heard." (Acts 4:19)

This is how those who experienced the love of the Lord feel, they cannot but speak the things which we have seen and heard! What does a believer experience in his relationship with God? He hears and sees a lot of things that "no eye has seen, nor ear heard" - a feeling of unutterable peace! Remember the words of the Lord, "... he who loves Me will be loved by My Father, and I will love him and manifest Myself to him... and We will come to him and make Our home with him." (John 14:21-23)

Thus, those whose hearts are ablazed with the love of the Lord cannot find rest except in serving the souls for which the Lord has shed His Honoured blood on the cross. Such believers can repeat with David the Prophet saying, "Surely I will not go into the chamber of my house, or go up to the comfort of my bed; I will not give sleep to my eyes or slumber to my eyelids, until I find a place for the Lord; A dwelling place for the Mighty One of Jacob." (Psalm 32:4)

Whoever does not believe in serving others is not a true Christian but rather a selfish person. In Christianity, there is nothing worse than selfishness as "Love does no harm to a neighbor; therefore love is the fulfillment of the law" (Romans 13:10) A true servant doesn't fear any dangers, troubles or death. "I saw under the altar the souls of those who had been slain for the word of God and for the testimony which they held, and they cried with a loud voice, saying, 'How long, O Lord, holy and true, until You judge and avenge our blood on those who dwell on the earth?' Then a white robe was given to each of them; and it was said to them that they should rest a little while longer, until both the number of their fellow servants and their brethren, who would be killed as they were, was completed." (Revelations 6:9,11)

When the Apostles departed from the presence of the council, they rejoiced that God has made them worthy to suffer shame for His Name. St Paul wrote to the priests of Ephesus saying, "And see, now I go bound in the spirit to Jerusalem, not knowing the things that will happen to me there, except that the Holy Spirit testifies in every city, saying that chains and tribulations await me. But none of these things move me; nor do I count my life dear to myself, so that I may finish my race with joy, and the ministry which I received from the Lord Jesus, to testify to the gospel of the grace of God." (Acts 20:22-24)

The Lord Jesus Christ came to the world as a messenger. " .... As the Father has sent Me, [so] I also send you." (John 20:21) "Just as the Son of Man did not come to be served, but to serve, and to give His life a ransom for many." (Matthew 20:28).

Jesus' last commandment on earth concerned service and the missionaries, "And He said to them, 'Go into all the world and preach the gospel to every creature.'" (Mark 16:15). Until now, God is commanding men, women, youth.... everyone – in different ways- to preach His Holy Name and His great love to mankind. He who refuses to obey God's commandments, in refusing to preach and serve others, is denying the great work done by God Himself for which He was incarnated.

THE SUBLIME HONOUR OF SERVICE

The New Testament promoted service as a means to get the hearts of people closer to God, to renew souls and attract them to the Kingdom of His love. Didn't the Lord Jesus bless the peace-makers calling them "children of God"? Therefore, we must walk through the world, setting peace between people and their Creator. It is only when we serve souls and bring them closer to God that we deserve to be called children of God.

St Paul clarifies this point saying, "Now all things are of God, who has reconciled us to Himself through Jesus Christ, and has given us the ministry of reconciliation... Now then, we are ambassadors for Christ, as though God were pleading through us: we implore you on Christ's behalf, be reconciled to God." (2 Corinthians 5: 18, 20), for "it is not the will of your Father who is in heaven that one of these little ones should perish." (Matthew 18: 14)

St Paul also highlights the sublime honour of service saying, "For we are God's fellow workers; you are God's field, you are God's building..." (1 Corinthians 3:9). How wonderful are the words "God's fellow workers"!!! How honourable to be working with God Himself!!!

How great is the word 'servant', it is a title deriving its honour from the Lord Himself, "just as the Son of Man did not come to be served, but to serve, and to give His life a ransom for many." (Matthew 20:28) Therefore, we can see that the Lord gives great honour to His honest servants, whether on earth or in heaven, "If anyone serves Me, let him follow Me; and where I am, there My servant will be also. If anyone serves Me, him My Father will honour." (John 12:26).

Daniel the Prophet also mentioned that, "Those who are wise shall shine like the brightness of the firmament, and those who turn many to righteousness like the stars forever and ever." (Daniel 12:3) Also, it is written about St Paul, "Now as he reasoned about righteousness, self-control, and the judgment to come, Felix was afraid and answered, 'Go away for now; when I have a convenient time I will call for you.'" (Acts 24:25), and so the judge was afraid of the imprisoned Paul!!

CONDITIONS OF A GOOD SERVANT

SPIRITUAL LEVEL

Wherever there is an honest and enthusiastic servant, there are plenty of fruits. A servant is a person who has a close relationship with God; a person whose heart is filled with His love. Therefore, such a servant cannot help but go around talking to others about the sweetness of the Lord.

A servant should be pure in his thoughts, dealings and general behaviour. He should be on a higher spiritual level than those whom he serves. A servant shows others the right path through his attitude much more than his words. His words only touch the heart of others if he has the right attitude. Isaiah the Prophet wrote about this saying, "O Zion, You who bring good tidings, get up into the high mountain..." (Isaiah 40:9). This means that those who teach others about heaven should have already left the low level of earthly concerns and be standing on high ground (as suggested through the 'mountain'). It is well-known that water flows from the upper springs to the lower valleys, but it can never go up from a low level!!

The hand which cleanses should be clean, "Be clean, you who bear the vessels of the Lord." (Isaiah 52:11). Who are those who bear the vessels of the Lord except those who bring souls closer to the Lord? Concerning St Paul, the Lord told Ananias, "Go, for he is a chosen vessel of Mine to bear My name before Gentiles, kings, and the children of Israel." (Acts 9:15).

St Paul assures us of these facts saying, "We give no offense in anything, that our ministry may not be blamed. But in all things we commend ourselves as ministers of God... by purity, by knowledge, by longsuffering, by kindness, by the Holy Spirit, by sincere love, by the word of truth, by the power of God, by the armor of righteousness on the right hand and on the left." (2 Corinthians 6:3-7)

He also wrote to his disciple Timothy saying,"Take heed to yourself and to the doctrine. Continue in them, for in doing this you will save both yourself and those who hear you." (1 Timothy 4:16). St Paul related Timothy's life to those whom he was serving since words from an impure soul can by no means touch the hearts of others.

PERSONALITY

A servant is the leader of the group he is serving.Thus, he has to have a certain personality to be fit for that kind of service. He has to enjoy a healthy mental, physical and psychological life. A servant should also always try to flee from sin as much as possible as he needs to be a model to others and not a stumbling block. For example, a servant should not use bad language, show a lack of self-control, be quick to anger or commit similar sins that are easily noticed and could potentially be a major stumbling block for others.

A servant must also have a high level of spiritual knowledge. He should not get confused when asked questions - ie. he should have the grace of speech. Solomons the wise says, "He who loves purity of heart and has grace on his lips, the king will be his friend."

(Proverbs 22:11). The concept of gracious speech is of great importance as it is written about the Lord Christ, "So all bore witness to Him, and marveled at the gracious words which proceeded out of His mouth. And they said, 'Is this not Joseph's son?'" (Luke 4:22)

St Matthew completed his recount of the Sermon on the Mount saying, "And so it was, when Jesus had ended these sayings, that the people were astonished at His teaching, for He taught them as one having authority, and not as the scribes" (Matthew 7:28-29).

The Lord Jesus gave us the authority of teaching as it is written, "Most assuredly, I say to you, he who believes in Me, the works that I do he will do also; and greater works than these he will do, because I go to My Father." (John 14:12) In the Acts of the Apostles, we read that from one sermon Peter gained 3000 souls, "Now it happened in Iconium that they went together to the synagogue of the Jews, and so spoke that a great multitude both of the Jews and of the Greeks believed." (Acts 14:1)

HIS AUTHORITY

The Lord Jesus gathered His twelve disiples before their first missionary journey and "gave them power and authority over all demons, and to cure diseases. He sent them to preach the kingdom of God and to heal the sick." (Luke 9:1-2). Ultimately, the secret weapon of a servant is this Divine authority. The Lord emphasised this strength after He told the disciples to "Take nothing for the journey, neither staff, nor bag, nor bread, nor money; and do not have two tunics apiece." (Luke 9:3). An honest servant can only obtain such Divine authority from his Teacher who "taught them as one having authority, and not as the scribes." (Mattew 7:29).

When Jeremiah the Prophet refrained from service, thinking he was too young, the Lord touched his mouth and said, "Behold, I have put My words in your mouth. See, I have this day set you over the nations and over the kingdoms, to root out and to pull down, to destroy and to throw down, to build and to plant." (Jeremiah 1:9-10). And again, "Therefore thus says the LORD God of hosts, 'Because you speak this word, behold, I will make My words in your mouth fire, and this people wood, and it shall devour them.'" (Jeremiah 5:14)

This is exactly what happened when St Peter attracted 3 000 souls to the Lord Christ through a single sermon. This is also comparable to the fire St Ephraim the Syrian saw coming out of the mouth of St Basil the Great while he was preaching to his congregation!!

Divine Authority is the key to success in service "For by fire and by His sword the Lord will judge all flesh; and the slain of the Lord shall be many" (Isaiah 66: 16). In other words, servants will conquer with "the sword of the Spirit, which is the word of God" (Ephesians 6:17)

His Responsibility

An honest servant feels that those whom he serves – who have come to know the Lord - are the subject for his joy, "For what is our hope, or joy, or crown of rejoicing? Is it not even you in the presence of our Lord Jesus Christ at His coming? For you are our glory and joy." (1 Thessolonians

2:19, 20). Such honest servants are also "….the seal of apostleship in the Lord." (1 Corinthians 9: 2) - that is, they reflect the truth and legacy of His mission.

An honest servant feels that he is responsible for every single soul before God and that is why he struggles without limits, "Him we preach, warning every man and teaching every man in all wisdom, that we may present every man perfect in Christ Jesus". (Colosians 1: 28) What makes him really feel responsible is the preciousness of the human soul - the price of the Blood of Jesus Christ. The more he values the human soul, the more he increases his service, tears, tolerance and sacrifices for the sake of their salvation.

An honest servant follows in the footsteps of the Lord Jesus. Our Saviour continues to pursue sheep that have gone astray for "It is not the will of the Father... that one of these little ones should perish." (Matthew 18: 14). We can feel this clearly in the life of St Paul the Apostle, who says, "nor do I count my life dear to myself, so that I may finish my race with joy, and the ministry which I received from the Lord Jesus, to testify to the gospel of the grace of God." (Acts 20: 24) We can also perceive the zeal of this honest servant as he felt responsible for every human soul, "Therefore I testify to you this day that I am innocent of the blood of all men." (Acts 20:26).

In his farewell speech to the priests of Ephesus, St Paul said,"... take heed to yourselves and to all the flock.... watch, and remember that for three years I did not cease to warn everyone night and day with tears." (Acts 20: 26-31). St Paul warned everyone with tears for he knew he had a great responsibility like his Master who "calls His sheep by name and leads them out." (John 1:3)

St Paul wrote to the Colossians saying, "To this end I also labor, striving according to His working which works mightily in me." (Colosians 1: 29). Also, in his catholic epistle, Timothy wrote "... I have fought the good fight, I have finished the race, I have kept the faith. Finally, there is laid up for me the crown of righteousness..." (2 Timothy 4: 7,8)

We read about many honest servants who feel responsible for every soul including St Macarius, Bishop of Faw. St Macarius used to weep in his sermons as he saw the sins of his congregation and feared that he would have to give an account of them before the Lord.

An honest servant worries about the sheep who have left the Great Shepherd who always calls out, "... come to Me... and you will find rest." However, it is important to note that an honest servant is always praying for the salvation of the world, not only the believers. This is because God sacrificed His Son so that ALL humanity can enjoy the blessings and joy of His salvation.

Choosing and Preparation of a Good Servant

Choosing A Servant

Choosing a servant is a difficult task. It is important to note that a regular person, who has no relationship with God, cannot be delegated to serve.This approach has two side-effects:

1. Those whom he is serving can never benefit from his service - he might even be a stumbling block to them

2. He will have a double personality: one will be pious and respectful (as during service) while the other is his usual self. Such a double personality can often lead to hypocrisy.

St John of the Ladder says, "Those who are still practicing repentance should not sit on the chairs of teachers". This suggests that those who start to serve before being spiritually mature will often talk a lot but the words coming out of their mouths are dead and cannot bring forth good fruit. Solomon the wise says, "If the clouds are full of rain, they empty themselves upon the earth." (Ecclesiastics 11:3). Explaining this verse, St Jerome says, "The clouds are the servants; if they are filled with spiritual water they can be useful to the land, but if they are dry with no water, then they are fulfilling the words of St Jude, 'They are clouds without water, carried about by the winds; late autumn trees without fruit.'"

The Bible tells us that choosing a servant requires a lot of fasting and praying. The Lord Jesus set Himself as an example for us as He prayed and fasted before choosing His twelve disciples. "Now it came to pass in those days that He went out to the mountain to pray, and continued all night in prayer... when it was day, He called His disciples... and from them He chose twelve whom He also named apostles" (Luke 6: 12,13). The disciples also fasted and prayed when they came to choose a disciple to replace Judas Iscariot, "And they prayed and said, 'You, O Lord, who know the hearts of all, show which of these two You have chosen'" (Acts 1:24).

We should not neither disregard nor be lenient in carrying out these conditions, no matter how urgent the need of a servant is, for the Lord Jesus knows our needs. "Then Jesus went about all the cities and villages, teaching in their synagogues, preaching the gospel of the kingdom, and healing every sickness and every disease among the people. But when He saw the multitudes, He was moved with compassion for them, because they were weary and scattered, like sheep having no shepherd..." Yet Jesus said to His disciples, "The harvest truly is plentiful, but the laborers are few." (Matthew 9:35- 37)

Although the Lord Jesus knew that the harvest is plentiful, He only chose twelve disciples to preach to the Kingdom of God to the whole world. The Lord also taught us how to deal with the increasing need of servants: "Therefore pray the Lord of the harvest to send out laborers into His harvest." (Matthew 9:38)

The Period of Preparing a Servant

After choosing a servant, we must start preparing him accordingly. The Lord Jesus started to serve at the age of thirty even though He was able to start at a much younger age: "All who heard Him were astonished at His understanding and answers." (Luke 2:47). The Lord also did not send His disciples to preach straight after His Glorious Resurrection but rather ordered them to wait forty days until they recieved power from above. No wonder Peter attracted 3000 souls on his first sermon!!!

We observe that the Lord's Servant's Preparation Class was as follows:

- the Teacher was the Master Jesus Christ

- the servants were His 12 disciples

- the teacher's resources were the miracles the Lord performed infront of them

- the classes were held everyday for more than three years

Sometimes we appoint the youth as servants thinking that this is the best way to get them closer to church. However, this approach is humiliating to the Lord and often results in poor service and a lot of trouble.

How to Prepare Servants

The curriculum should include:

1- Bible Study, theology, rites and church history- It is important that the servant is very knowledge in such areas as they will have to answer the questions of those whom he is serving. The age/level of those whom a particular servant will serve should also be taken into consideration.

2- Some psychology and general education- This is important as it will help the servant relate and deal effectively with the problems of those whom he is serving. The servant should take into consideration the physical and psychological abilities of those whom he is serving in order to effectively engage with his students and prepare a lesson that will they will find both beneficial and enjoyable. A servant should also be trained to use different teaching aids and strategies.

3- The servant should also be given a chance to give a Sunday School lesson while under the supervision of an experienced servant.

The servant should always be filled with the spirit of discipleship. Christianity is originally based on the spirit of discipleship, as the Lord Jesus said to His disciples before His Ascension, "Go therefore and make disciples of all the nations... teaching them to observe all things that I have commanded you..." (Matthew 28:19, 20). In following His commandment, the Church has become strong with believers increasing in virtue and knowledge. Discipleship is the key to building souls. It is founded on obedience, humility, love and holy zeal.

SUPERFICIAL SERVICE

ITS DANGERS

Superficiality is a serious disease. It never leads to any progress or development in any aspect of our lives. Thus, consider how dangerous superficial service would be. The Lord Jesus ordered Simon Peter to throw the fishing nets into the deep water. When the disciple obeyed, he caught plenty of fish. Similarly, if we listen to God's voice from the depth of our hearts, He will pour upon us His blessings and goodness.

Superficiality in service is a product of superficiality in one's spiritual life.

SIGNS OF SUPERFICIALITY

1- Caring about the outward appearance of the service- Often servants are too preoccupied by the outward appearances that they are negligent of the quality of their service. Some servants only care about starting a new service despite the fact that they are neither ready nor prepared to take on this new service. Often such a service is rushed and may result in a failure. For example, a Sunday school teacher may quickly answer a question incorrectly, not out of bad intentions, but out of ignorance.

2- Going church, reading the Holy Bible, fasting and praying out of routine- Our Lord Jesus asked us all to lead a life of perfection, "Therefore you shall be perfect, just as your Father in heaven is perfect." (Matthew 5: 48). We are also asked to continuously grow in grace "... till we all come to the unity of the faith and of the knowledge of the Son of God, to a perfect man, to the measure of the stature of the fullness of Christ." (Ephesus 4:13).

St Paul clarifies that everyone (not only those who have consecrated their lives for worship) is asked to live a life of perfection: "Him we preach, warning every man and teaching every man in all wisdom, that we may present every man perfect in Christ Jesus..." (Colosians 1:29).

Some people think that a successful service is all about the number of children attending Sunday School, or attending a sermon, or partaking of the Holy Communion... etc. But the Lord Jesus tells us "... Nevertheless, do not rejoice in this..." (Luke 10:20). Superficiality in Christianity resembles the seeds "...[which] fell on stony places, where they did not have much earth; and they immediately sprang up because they had no depth of earth." (Matthew 13:5)

STRENGTH IN THE LIFE OF A SERVANT

LOVE

Love gives servants the power to grow in a closer personal relationship with the Lord and to serve in His holy vineyard. When Satan sought to divide the growing church in Corinth, St Paul wrote to the Corinthians about love (in Chapter 13). A servant must be well aware that any good deed or virtue which is void of love is rejected by God - once they grumble or growl, their toil and labour becomes vain.

No one can resist the power of love. It is love that lifted the Son of God on the Cross... it is love that transformed Saul the persecutor into the greater preacher St Paul ... it is love that stripped Saul from the robe of a Pharisee and clothed him with the robe of an Apostle... it is love that opposed Saul of Tarsus by the gates of Damascus and transformed him into a proud "prisoner of the Lord". Truly, St Paul can rightly claim that "the love of Christ surrounds us."

Love solves all problems encountered in service... It was the reason why the apostles willingly struggled to preach the Gospel. Love turns the bitterness of persecution into sweetness. No iron bars nor prison cells can bind love. A heart full of love enpowers a servant with increased zeal for the joy and salvation of others - he cannot rest as long as they are held captive by Satan. This is clearly seen through Daniel the Prophet who "Set [his] face towards the Lord God to make request by prayer and supplications, with fasting, sackcloth, and ashes...." (Daniel 9:3).

Love was the reason why Nehemiah sought to re-build the walls of Jerusalem: "Come and let us build the wall of Jerusalem, that we may no longer be a reproach." (Nehemiah 2:17) Jerusalem is the Church which is in great need for zealous servants like Nehemiah... The Lord Jesus wept over Jerusalem "Now as He drew near, He saw the city and wept over it, saying, 'If you had known, even you, especially in this your day, the things that make for your peace! But now they are hidden from your eyes.'" (Luke 19:41)

We frequently read of St Paul's zeal towards the salvation of the souls: "Who is weak, and I am not weak? Who is made to stumble, and I do not burn with indignation?" (2 Corinthians 11:29). "For I could wish that I myself were accursed from Christ for my brethren, my countrymen according to the flesh." (Romans 9:3). St Paul was imprisoned in Caesarea and his only concern was not his release but rather the salvation of those imprisoned with him. When King Agrippa said, "You almost persuade me to become a Christian", his answer was, "I would to God that not only you, but also all who hear me today, might become both almost and altogether such as I am, except for these chains." (Acts 26:28-29)

We also read about the tears St Paul shed in his service. When he farewells the priests of Ephesus, he says: "Therefore watch, and remember that for three years I did not cease to warn everyone night and day with tears." (Acts 20:31) Tears are a sign of love, holy zeal and warm affections. No one can overcome tears "Turn your eyes away from me, for they have overcome me." (Song of Songs 6:5)

Service is founded on love. Love helps us dissolve divisions inside the church that destroy and weaken it. St Paul says, "Love suffers long and is kind; love does not envy; love does not parade itself, is not puffed up; does not behave rudely, does not seek its own, is not provoked, thinks no evil; does not rejoice in iniquity, but rejoices in the truth; bears all things, believes all things, hopes all things, endures all things..." Finally the Apostle crowns love with the top of all virtues, " Love never fails." (1 Corinthians 13). Those who do not love have never known God, as it is clearly written "God is Love".

FAITH

God granted faith the strength to work and to take, the Holy Bible is full of the promises to those who have faith and its power, as well as the biography of the heroes of faith and the work of God with them.

When the Lord sent His disciples in their early missionaries, He commanded them, "Provide neither gold nor silver nor copper in your money belts, nor bag for your journey, nor two tunics, nor sandals, nor staffs; for a worker is worthy of his food." (Matt.10: 9,10), but at the same time He provided them with His Divine authority and they performed great miracles through believing in His Holy Name (Luke 10: 17)

Apart from the blessings of faith, lack of faith is a great sin (Rom. 14: 23); faith in God is to believe Him and His promises, disbelieving is a great insult to God, as it is written, "But without faith it is impossible to please Him..." (Heb.11: 6)

Faith never gets old, the promises of God have the same strength at all times. Any person who has the same faith as the early preachers can do the same miracles or even greater than what they had done, the Lord Jesus Himself says, "Most assuredly, I say to you, he who believes in Me, the works that I do he will do also; and greater works than these he will do..." (John 14: 12)

Beware of fear, hesitation and doubt; for these are the enemies of faith. According to God's orders, Moses sent 12 spies to the land of Canaan, amongst them were Caleb and Joshua. After 40 days all the 12 came back, 10 of them started spreading fear, doubt and the spirit of weakness and defeat among the people, talking about the giants who inhabit this land and Amalek, as for Caleb and Joshua they said, "Let us go up at once and take possession, for we are well able to overcome it...Only do not rebel against the Lord, nor fear the people of the land, for they are our bread; their protection has departed from them, and the Lord is with us. Do not fear them." (Num. 13, 14)

The same is happening nowadays, lots of people believe that the current of evil in this world is stronger than their abilities, we are in need for the faith of Caleb and Joshua, of the young shepherd David who killed Goliath through the power of the Lord of hosts, God is the same yesterday, today and forever... He never changes!

If the harvest is plenty and the workers are few, we are in sheer need of honest servants who believe in their mission and in the power of Him of whom they are preaching... we do not look at the number of servants but at the quality.

Gideon defeated the Midianites, the Amalekites and the people of the East with 300 men, they were "...coming in as numerous as locusts; both they and their camels were without number..." Gideon had an army of around 32,000 fighters, but when he knew that the army of the Midianites were greater than his, he feared and doubted, so the Lord said to him, "The people who are with you are too many for Me to give the Midianites into their hands, lest Israel claim glory for itself against Me, saying, 'My own hand has saved me.' Now therefore, proclaim in the hearing of the people, saying, 'Whoever is fearful and afraid, let him turn and depart at once from Mount Gilead.'" And twenty-two thousand of the people returned, and ten thousand remained. But the Lord said to Gideon, "The people are still too many; bring them down to the water, and I will test them for you there." After the testing, "Then the Lord said to Gideon, "By the three hundred men who lapped I will save you, and deliver the Midianites into your hand." (Judges 7)

Let's get rid of those who hide their fear and doubt in the robe of wisdom and protection, let's believe in the promises of the Lord more than believing in what those reluctant people say. We have to read a lot about the men of God who, "who through faith subdued kingdoms, worked righteousness, obtained promises, stopped the mouths of lions, quenched the violence of fire, escaped the edge of the sword, out of weakness were made strong, became valiant in battle, turned to flight the armies of the aliens." (Heb. 11: 33, 34)

At the wedding of Cana of Galilee, when the Mother of God noticed that they had ran out of wine, "His mother said to the servants, "Whatever He says to you, do it." (John 2: 5). We need to keep strong hold of obeying in faith till the end. When the servants obeyed, it was the first miracle performed by the Lord Jesus. When we obey the Lord with deep faith in the service, we will witness miracles taking place.

ROLE-MODEL

Christianity is a preaching missionary, it was spread through role-models more than sermons and teachings. Through their love to their God, their holy fruitful life and their steadfast faith, they were able to glorify their Lord and defeat the forts of evil and paganism, fulfilling the commandment of their Lord Jesus Christ, "Let your light so shine before men, that they may see your good works and glorify your Father in heaven." (Matt.5: 16)

If this is the case with the normal believer who is a member of the church, what about the pastors and servants who are responsible for being a role model to those whom they are serving?!

The Lord Jesus Christ, the Greatest Teacher says, "Learn from Me...", also "And for their sakes I sanctify Myself...." (John 17: 19). His servant and apostle Paul says, "Imitate me..." and commands his disciple Timothy the Bishop, "Take heed to yourself and to the doctrine. Continue in them, for in doing this you will save both yourself and those who hear you." (1 Tim. 4: 16)

The importance of being a role model as a servant

is clear in the Lord's words through Ezekiel the Prophet, "Indeed I Myself will search for My sheep and seek them out... Is it too little for you to have eaten up the good pasture, that you must tread down with your feet the residue of your pasture—and to have drunk of the clear waters, that you must foul the residue with your feet? And as for My flock, they eat what you have trampled with your feet, and they drink what you have fouled with your feet." (Ez. 34: 11, 18)

Here, the Lord points to the servants and pastors who are not living according to the teachings that they deliver to those whom they serve. The Holy Inspiration declared this point very clearly saying, "tread down with your feet" i.e. treading down with their feet on the teachings.

In this case, those whom they are serving are affected by the bad role model rather than the teachings, as the Lord said about the Levites, "Because they ministered to them before their idols and caused the house of Israel to fall into iniquity, therefore I have raised My hand in an oath against them," says the Lord God, "that they shall bear their iniquity." (Ez.44: 12)

At church, nothing is worse and more harmful than someone who appears holy while commiting evil things. Those who do not deserve to be servants – inspite of its numerous blessings - should refrain, listening to the Lord's words, "Whoever causes one of these little ones who believe in Me to sin, it would be better for him if a millstone were hung around his neck , and he were drowned in the depth of the sea." (Matt.18: 6)

The servant or pastor's sermon or teaching should

be about the cream of his personal life, as a servant once answered someone who asked him; 'How long have you been preparing for this sermon?' And he answered '40 years', i.e. all his personal experiences during the past 40 years of his life.

Prayers

A very well known spiritual fact is that a Christian person is totally dead if he does not pray, he is deceiving himself if he thinks there is another door to receive the Divine support except that of prayers!! Much more what about a servant, the secret of power in our lives as believers comes from prayers, and it is the same in the lives of strong servants.

Nothing except prayers makes a servant who is serving God, it is a guarantee that his service will be with the "evidence of spirit and power". The Lord's commandment to His disciples before His Ascension was, "Behold, I send the Promise of My Father upon you; but tarry in the city of Jerusalem until you are endued with power from on high." (Luke 24: 49)

These words were a warning not to dare and start the service and preaching before getting this power. The Lord's promise was fulfilled and that happened on the day of the Pentecost. It is explained in the Book of Acts how they gained this power, "These all continued with one accord in prayer and supplication…" (Acts 1: 14)

The secret of the strong service and preaching lies in the work of the Holy Spirit which accompanies the words. Prayer is the means to achieve it, praying with the spirit.

"The power from on high" is not granted except through the living prayers ascending to above. Thus, the servant needs a strong power for his salvation and for the service affecting others.

The service at the early church was progressing through the strength and push of prayers, and so "the word of the Lord grew mightily and prevailed." (Acts 19: 20). All the problems were solved through prayers. Miracles and wonders were performed through prayers, the basics of faith were strengthened and established through the power of prayers.

All the kings, emperors and governors who opposed the faith were destroyed through prayers, heresies were void through the power of prayer.

When the disciples were facing so many opponents at their preaching mission, they all kept praying in one accord , "Now, Lord, look on their threats, and grant to Your servants that with all boldness they may speak Your word,". The result was: "And when they had prayed, the place where they were assembled together was shaken; and they were all filled with the Holy Spirit, and they spoke the word of God with boldness."(Acts 4: 29-31)

When Herod the King imprisoned Peter, the iron gates of the prison opened to him of its own accord because "constant prayer was offered to God for him by the church."(Acts 12: 5)

The same happened with Paul and Silas when the gates of the prison were opened and the prisoners' ties were all released because of their prayers and praises, and that was a reason for the belief of the keeper of the prison and all his household. (Acts 16: 25-33)

Although the number of the believers was increasing, leading to more responsibility laid on the disciples, they never neglected prayers.

When they gathered to discuss the issue, they said, "Then the twelve summoned the multitude of the disciples and said, "It is not desirable that we should leave the word of God and serve tables. Therefore, brethren, seek out from among you seven men of good reputation, full of the Holy Spirit and wisdom, whom we may appoint over this business; but we will give ourselves continually to prayer and to the ministry of the word." (Acts 6: 2-4)

Here notice the priorities: Regular prayer comes before service.

We mentioned previously that the servant should pray for his salvation and those whom he is serving. St. Paul the great preacher and honest servant is calling us to follow his footsteps, "Imitate me, just as I also imitate Christ. (1 Cor. 11: 1)

Here are some of the fiery prayers of this honest apostle:

"...night and day praying exceedingly that we may see your face and perfect what is lacking in your faith" (1 Thes.3: 10)

"Therefore I also, after I heard of your faith in the Lord Jesus and your love for all the saints, do not cease to give thanks for you, making mention of you in my prayers" (Eph. 1: 15, 16)

"For this reason I bow my knees to the Father of our Lord Jesus Christ, from whom the whole family in heaven and earth is named, that He would grant you, according to the riches of His glory, to be strengthened with might through His Spirit in the inner man, that Christ may dwell in your hearts through faith; that you, being rooted and grounded in love…" (Eph.3: 14-17)

"I thank my God upon every remembrance of you, always in every prayer of mine making request for you all with joy……For God is my witness, how greatly I long for you all with the affection of Jesus Christ. And this I pray, that your love may abound still more and more in knowledge and all discernment" (Phil.1: 3-9)

"We give thanks to the God and Father of our Lord Jesus Christ, praying always for you, since we heard of your faith in Christ Jesus and of your love for all the saints…… For this reason we also, since the day we heard it, do not cease to pray for you, and to ask that you may be filled with the knowledge of His will in all wisdom and spiritual understanding;" (Col.1: 3-9)

As for encouraging those whom we serve to pray for the service, we have many examples in most of St. Paul's Epistles; testifying to the faith of this saint that prayers are essential for service and preaching:

"Now I beg you, brethren, through the Lord Jesus Christ, and through the love of the Spirit, that you strive together with me in prayers to God for me that I may be delivered from those in Judea who do not believe, and that my service for Jerusalem may be acceptable to the saints" (Rom.15: 30,31) "you also helping together in prayer for us, that thanks may be given by many persons on our behalf for the gift granted to us through many." (2 Cor.1: 11)

"praying always with all prayer and supplication in the Spirit, being watchful to this end with all perseverance and supplication for all the saints and for me, that utterance may be given to me, that I may open my mouth boldly to make known the mystery of the gospel," (Eph.6: 18,19)

"Continue earnestly in prayer, being vigilant in it with thanksgiving; meanwhile praying also for us, that God would open to us a door for the word, to speak the mystery of Christ, for which I am also in chains," (Col.4: 2,3)

"Finally, brethren, pray for us, that the word of the Lord may run swiftly and be glorified, just as it is with you," (2 Thes. 3:1)

SELF-DENIAL

Self-denial is the strong foundation for building a servant's personality and service. After comparing between worldly races and spiritual struggle, declaring that a believer wins at the end, St Paul says: "Do you not know that those who run in a race all run, but one receives the prize.....Therefore I run thus: not with uncertainty. Thus I fight: not as one who beats the air. But I discipline my body and bring it into subjection, lest, when I have preached to others, I myself should become disqualified." (1 Cor. 9: 24-27)

Someone might think could this great preacher and saint be disqualified?! But this is mentioned for our benefit so that we might test ourselves and care about our salvation even if we've been servants for so many years we have to always feel that we've just started. This should be the strong foundation for every servant concerning his service.

When God called Jeremiah to become a prophet he apologized because of his young age, yet the Lord encouraged him with Divine promises, "Then the Lord put forth His hand and touched my mouth, and the Lord said to me:

" Behold, I have put My words in your mouth. See, I have this day set you over the nations and over the kingdoms, to root out and to pull down, to destroy and to throw down, to build and to plant."(Jer 1: 9-10)

"Therefore thus says the Lord God of hosts: "Because you speak this word, behold, I will make My words in your mouth fire, and this people wood, and it shall devour them."(Jer.5: 14)

Thus we should never feel that we are fit for the service no matter our history of service or our education. We should rather feel that the success achieved is all because of the words which the Lord has put in our mouths, as St. Paul says: "Not that we are sufficient of ourselves to think of anything as being from ourselves, but our sufficiency is from God, who also made us sufficient as ministers of the new covenant, not of the letter but of the Spirit; for the letter kills, but the Spirit gives life." (2 Cor. 3: 5,6)

The same happened with Isaiah the Prophet, "So I said: "Woe is me, for I am undone! Because I am a man of unclean lips…. Then one of the seraphim flew to me, having in his hand a live coal which he had taken with the tongs from the altar. And he touched my mouth with it, and said: " Behold, this has touched your lips; Your iniquity is taken away, and your sin purged." Also I heard the voice of the Lord, saying "Whom shall I send, and who will go for Us?" Then I said, "Here am I! Send me." And He said, "Go, and tell this people…" (Is.6: 5-9)

My dear servants, you should feel that the Lord has touched your lips with His pure hands, especially when you are regularly partaking of the Holy Body and Precious Blood, which are the live coal in Isaiah's words. Everytime you are serving and talking about the Lord, make sure that He has put His words in your mouth.

FILLED WITH THE HOLY SPIRIT

God is Spirit, so all those who want to serve Him have to be filled with the Spirit, "It is the Spirit who gives life; the flesh profits nothing. The words that I speak to you are spirit, and they are life" (John 6: 63). What really matters is the power of the Spirit accompanying the words, but not the words themselves, "For our gospel did not come to you in word only, but also in power, and in the Holy Spirit and in much assurance, as you know what kind of men we were among you for your sake." (1 Thes.1: 5)

"For the word of God is living and powerful, and sharper than any two-edged sword, piercing even to the division of soul and spirit, and of joints and marrow, and is a discerner of the thoughts and intents of the heart." (Heb.4: 12). In his Epistle to the Ephesians, St. Paul calls the word of God "the Sword of the Spirit" (Eph. 6:17).

Again, St.Paul clarifies this fact by saying: "And I,

brethren, when I came to you, did not come with excellence of speech or of wisdom declaring to you the testimony of God. For I determined not to know anything among you except Jesus Christ and Him crucified. I was with you in weakness, in fear, and in much trembling. And my speech and my preaching were not with persuasive words of human wisdom, but in demonstration of the Spirit and of power, that your faith should not be in the wisdom of men but in the power of God."(1Cor.2: 1-5)

The convincing words of human wisdom is logic and philosophy. St. Paul was a prime philosopher of Christianity, so he would have rather addressed the believers in Corinth with philosophical terms and logic, yet he didn't; because preaching about the Kingdom of God is not to be spread in such a way, but he preached "in demonstration of the Spirit and of power". So what is the demonstration of the Spirit??

The mind convinces the mind and the Spirit convinces the spirit. When the Spirit talks He has His special way that is of the day of the Pentecost. How eloquent and powerful was Peter the Apostle's words on the day of Pentecost, "Now when they heard this, they were cut to the heart, and said to Peter and the rest of the apostles, "Men and brethren, what shall we do?" (Acts 2: 37); and the answer was to "Repent". This is the demonstration of the Spirit through which the Church carries out the will of its Master and Saviour, to preach to the entire world and humanity. The demonstration of the Spirit does not need arguing or conversation, it is irresistible, "for I will give you a mouth and wisdom which all your adversaries will not be able to contradict or resist." (Luke 21: 15)

What took place on the day of the Pentecost during St. Peter's sermon was the demonstration of the Spirit. The catechumens who were accepting this new invitation did not argue or ask for a proof because the Spirit worked in them so powerfully and cut their hearts.

St. Paul says that his preaching was "in demonstration of the Spirit and of power", the power he is talking about is the same power promised by the Lord to His disciples, as He commanded them to stay in Jerusalem "until you are endued with power from on high." (Luke 24: 49). It is also written, "But you shall receive power when the Holy Spirit has come upon you;" (Acts 1: 8).

STUDING THE WORD OF GOD

The Word of God is a great spring where the power of God is stored. All the honest and successful servants built their lives and service on the basis of the word of God, as the Lord says, "Is not My word like a fire?" says the Lord, " And like a hammer that breaks the rock in pieces?" (Jer. 23: 29). Also, "the seed is the word of God" (Luke 8: 11)

If the word of God is so essential to the normal believer as a spiritual daily food for his spiritual development, what about the servant, whom sometimes is called 'servant of the word of God'. He has to study the word of God to know His will and way and pass it to those whom he is serving, to know the nature of human beings and how to win the souls. All the facts that he needs to talk about are recorded in the Holy Bible, a servant doesn't need to excel in many subjects, but he needs to study the word of God. St. Paul addresses his disciple Timothy saying, "Till I come, give attention to reading, to exhortation, to doctrine. Do not neglect the gift that is in you, which was given to you by prophecy with the laying on of the hands of the eldership. Meditate on these things; give yourself entirely to them, that your progress may be evident to all." (1 Tim.4: 13-15)

The most important book for a servant to deeply study is the Holy Bible. He could read many other spiritual books and excerpts from them, but the Holy Bible is the base. After Joshua became the leader of the children of Israel, the Lord instructed him saying, "This Book of the Law shall not depart from your mouth, but you shall meditate in it day and night, that you may observe to do according to all that is written in it. For then you will make your way prosperous, and then you will have good success." (Joshua 1: 8)

The Holy Bible is "given by inspiration of God, and is profitable for doctrine, for reproof, for correction, for instruction in righteousness, that the man of God may be complete, thoroughly equipped for every good work." (2 Tim.3: 16, 17)

From this beneficial book the servant of God could shield himself with the appropriate weapon to defeat his enemies. The Lord Jesus defeated Satan when he tried to tempt Him with the word of God. If we use and depend on the word of God in our service, we will find that "the word of God is living and powerful, and sharper than any two-edged sword, piercing even to the division of soul and spirit, and of joints and marrow, and is a discerner of the thoughts and intents of the heart." (Heb.4: 12)

Beware of studying the word of God just for the sake

of preaching to others, but our aim has to be primarily our own sufficiency and fullness, so that it becomes part of our spiritual structure, thus it will have a wonderful effect on others due to the work of the Holy Spirit.

In addition to studying the Holy Bible, the servant should be up to date with nowadays modern technology and general knowledge, to be able to answer different questions, inquiries or life problems that might be asked by his children.

DETACHMENT

Detachment is a Christian virtue which should be ornamenting all believers, here we mean getting rid of the love of the world in all its forms, "Do you not know that friendship with the world is enmity with God?" (James 4: 4). This virtues differs in levels from one believer to the other, some might reach the extent of selling all their possession, and this used to happen in the early church. The disciples also declared their belief in this virtue by saying to the Lord Jesus, "See, we have left all and followed You." (Matt.19: 27)

All the believers are asked to obtain this virtue, especially the servants, as this virtue depends on uniting the heart to the love of God. David the prophet asked God in his prayers to "Unite my heart to fear Your name." (Ps. 86: 11).

The heart sometimes is pulled between many desires, although the commandment is "My son, give Me your heart." (Prov. 23: 26); and " 'You shall love the Lord your God with all your heart, with all your soul, and with all your mind" (Matt. 22: 37).

The greatest calamity and danger appears when the heart is divided, thus a servant starts justifying his negligence and weakened love towards God. David the Prophet prays saying, "Do not incline my heart to any evil thing, to practice wicked works with men who work iniquity; and do not let me eat of their delicacies." (Ps. 141: 4).

Let's give the Lord our hearts and always be united with Him. The Divine Scripture says, "For the eyes of the Lord run to and fro throughout the whole earth, to show Himself strong on behalf of those whose heart is loyal to Him." (2 Chr. 16: 9)

Talking about asceticism; after graduation, the youth who is volunteering to serve gets attracted to the world. He tries to work for extra hours, aims at a higher position or greater salary or studying for a higher degree and so on. Gradually he starts neglecting his service and in a few years he is dragged off the life of God and His service.

Here we are not discouraging ambitions, but maybe this life style is appropriate for a normal Christian person and here we need to declare that we do not oppose ambition and progress, but we are addressing the few number of people whose hearts are inflamed with the love of God and His children, devoting their time and love for service. There is no doubt God will reward such honest servants who preferred His service rather than positions, authorities and material issues.

This is about the volunteer servants, but there are consecrated servants yet they are not living the lovely experience of detachment. They might have given up their positions for the sake of the service, yet they did not give their whole heart totally to the Lord. Here we might address the same words said to Ananias by St. Peter to these servants. "While it remained, was it not your own....Tell me whether you sold the land for so much?" (Acts 5: 4-8). So, give a self account and think; before consecrating your life to the Lord was it not all yours? Did you keep some of the love of the world? Did you take from the price of the field, which is your heart and life?

In the miracle of feeding the five thousand, the disciples said to the Lord, "We have here only five loaves and two fish." He said, "Bring them here to Me." (Matt.14: 17, 18). The Lord took the five loaves and two fish and blessed them feeding everyone, and there were left overs as well. The Lord asked for all what they had, and they gave it, thus the miracle of blessing and overflowing happened. So they all ate and were filled, and they took up twelve baskets full of the fragments that remained. What would of happened if one of the disciples had little faith and kept some for himself?!

KINDNESS AND LOVE

There is no doubt that love and kindness towards those whom we are serving helps in building them spiritually as love is one of the main Christian characteristics. Jesus used to consider the evil ones as ill and in need of help to cure and so He attracted millions of people through His love and kindness. St. Paul writes, "love edifies" (1 Cor.8: 1)... and the Lord Jesus was a friend to the sinners and tax collectors as it is written, "Then Jesus went about all the cities and villages, teaching in their synagogues, preaching the gospel of the kingdom, and healing every sickness and every disease among the people. But when He saw the multitudes, He was moved with compassion for them, because they were weary and scattered, like sheep having no shepherd." (Matt.9: 35,36)

Love and compassion were also the characteristics of the disciples and apostles of the Lord, as St. Paul writes, "Nor did we seek glory from men, either from you or from others, when we might have made demands as apostles of Christ. But we were gentle among you, just as a nursing mother cherishes her own children. So, affectionately longing for you, we were well pleased to impart to you not only the gospel of God, but also our own lives, because you had become dear to us." (1 Thes.2: 6-8). Also, "Brethren, if a man is overtaken in any trespass, you who are spiritual restore such a one in a spirit of gentleness, considering yourself lest you also be tempted." (Gal.6: 1).

Harshness with a sinner is not beneficial, it might rather lead him to stray from God and the church, "And a servant of the Lord must not quarrel but be gentle to all, able to teach, patient, in humility correcting those who are in opposition, if God perhaps will grant them repentance, so that they may know the truth, and that they may come to their senses and escape the snare of the devil, having been taken captive by him to do his will." (2 Tim.2: 24-26)

King David dismissed Absalom as the latter rebelled against his father, to the extent that he wanted to kill him yet David never neglected him as a son and he still loved him, and when he ordered his army to fight Absalom, he commanded them saying,"Deal gently for my sake with the young man Absalom."(2 Sam.18: 5). Here David is a resemblance of the Lord Jesus Christ and Absalom is a resemblance of any rebellion sinner. It is the same feelings of the Lord towards the wicked and the sinner, He deals gently with them and commands us to deal gently with them.

Absalom was killed by the old hard-hearted Joab inspite of his master's command and there are lots of people like Joab, while Jesus is ordering us to gently treat the sinners, there comes a Joab to kill them harshly thus breaking the Lord's heart, exactly as David's heart when he knew about the death of his son Absalom.

WISDOM AND RESILIENCE

How sweet is the word 'wisdom', "For wisdom is better than rubies, and all the things one may desire cannot be compared with her." (Prov.8: 11). The Lord Jesus is pleased to be called wisdom, "but we preach Christ..... Christ the power of God and the wisdom of God." (1 Cor.1: 23,24), "to the knowledge of the mystery of God, both of the Father and of Christ, in whom are hidden all the treasures of wisdom and knowledge."

The Lord Jesus who, "increased in wisdom and stature, and in favor with God and men" (Luke 2: 52) commands us to "be wise as serpents and harmless as doves." (Matt.10: 16)

He promises His disciples and children at the time of tribulations, "for I will give you a mouth and wisdom which all your adversaries will not be able to contradict or resist." (Luke 21: 15). He was so wise answering those who wanted to make disputes between Him and the ruling authorities, "And He said to them, "Render therefore to Caesar the things that are Caesar's, and to God the things that are God's." (Matt. 22: 21)

Some of the problems which we face at church and service are the result of dealing unwisely and being unflexible with issues. We always stick to our own view, thinking that the truth is by our side not the other, and the result is division, failure and destruction. This does not mean to give up our principles, but we have to be wise for the sake of the unity of the church and the salvation of souls. This is very clear in the words of the great philosopher and wise teacher St. Paul the Apostle, "For though I am free from all men, I have made myself a servant to all, that I might win the more; and to the Jews I became as a Jew, that I might win Jews; to those who are under the law, as under the law, that I might win those who are under the law; to those who are without law, as without law (not being without law toward God, but under law toward Christ, that I might win those who are without law; to the weak I became as weak, that I might win the weak. I have become all things to all men, that I might by all means save some. Now this I do for the gospel's sake, that I may be partaker of it with you." (1 Cor.9: 19-23).

The explanation of these words is very clear that the apostle did not resist all these categories which he served at the beginning or abolished their beliefs, but through them, and in a wise attitude, he led them to believe in the Lord Christ.

Two wonderful incidents for St. Paul prove these words: One with the Jews and the other with the pagans. Although he opposed the idea of the pagans becoming Jews first then Christians, and although he delivered the decisions of the Ecumenical Council in Jerusalem to the other churches (Acts 15), yet after meeting Timothy in Derbe and Lystra and knowing that he wished to go out for service with St. Paul, it is written, "Then he came to Derbe and Lystra. And behold, a certain disciple was there, named Timothy, the son of a certain Jewish woman who believed, but his father was Greek. He was well spoken of by the brethren who were at Lystra and Iconium. Paul wanted to have him go on with him. And he took him and circumcised him because of the Jews who were in that region, for they all knew that his father was Greek." (Acts 16: 1-3)

In Athens - the hometown of philosophers - and in the middle of the Areopagus and all the philosophers and Athenians, he started his speech by wisely saying, "Then Paul stood in the midst of the Areopagus and said, "Men of Athens, I perceive that in all things you are very religious; for as I was passing through and considering the objects of your worship, I even found an altar with this inscription: TO THE UNKNOWN GOD. Therefore, the One whom you worship without knowing, Him I proclaim to you: God, who made the world and everything in it, since He is Lord of heaven and earth." (Acts 17: 22-24)

It is very strange that few verses earlier it is written about Paul that, "Now while Paul waited for them at Athens, his spirit was provoked within him when he saw that the city was given over to idols." (Acts 17: 16)

Wisdom is a deep rooted Christian characteristic which every servant should have. When the early church decided to appoint helpers to serve with the Apostles, the condition was that they should be "filled with the Holy Spirit and wisdom" (Acts 6; 3), and that was fulfilled, because when some opposers started to argue with Stephen, " they were not able to resist the wisdom and the Spirit by which he spoke." (Acts 6: 10)

Wisdom was the commandment of all the Apostles. St. Paul the "wise master builder" (1 Cor.3: 10) commands the believers of Colossians to "Walk in wisdom toward those who are outside, redeeming the time." (Col. 4: 5), and "Let the word of Christ dwell in you richly in all wisdom," (Col.3: 16) also telling the Corinthians, "But be that as it may, I did not burden you. Nevertheless, being crafty, I caught you by cunning!" (2 Cor. 12-16)

St. James assures these words, "If any of you lacks wisdom, let him ask of God, who gives to all liberally and without reproach, and it will be given to him." (James 1: 5)

Wisdom is a basic in the service, it walks side by side with winning the souls as it is written, "And he who wins souls is wise" (Prov. 11: 30).

The Lord Jesus clarified this point when he connected catching fish to winning the souls when talking to Simon Peter in Luke Chapter 5, as both need wisdom, caution and experience.

Our servants need lots of wisdom and resilience, not the worldly wisdom which is "earthly, sensual, demonic…. But the wisdom that is from above is first pure, then peaceable, gentle, willing to yield, full of mercy and good fruits, without partiality and without hypocrisy." (James 3: 15-17)

We would like to attract the leaders of Sunday School not to leave the young servants to take decisions by themselves, because they might still lean on the wisdom of this world, as Elihu says: "I said, 'Age should speak, and multitude of years should teach wisdom." (Job 32: 7)

CONCENTRATION:

There are lots of servants, out of their desire to serve, engage in many fields in different places, which leads to a lose in concentration, consequently to failure and despair even in the servant's general life especially spiritually. If we are students or in a working position, we have to also be honest in carrying out these responsibilities, not justifying our negligence because of serving God; otherwise "we hinder the gospel of Christ." (1 Cor.9: 12)

For these people the time of service is limited, and so they should use it wisely, neither neglecting the service nor their other responsibilities, just to be honest and moderate.

Our Lord Jesus Christ says, "For what profit is it to a man if he gains the whole world, and loses his own soul? Or what will a man give in exchange for his soul?" (Matt.16: 26)

St. Paul also says; "But I discipline my body and bring it into subjection, lest, when I have preached to others, I myself should become disqualified. (1 Cor.9: 27).So, it is possible that the servant who is preaching about salvation for others would himself be rejected at the end because of his reluctance.

Let's always remember the Lord's words, "Many will

say to Me in that day, 'Lord, Lord, have we not prophesied in Your name, cast out demons in Your name, and done many wonders in Your name?' And then I will declare to them, 'I never knew you; depart from Me, you who practice lawlessness!' (Matt.7: 22, 23)

The words 'I never knew you' points to the fact that these people never had a personal relationship with the Lord. It is really astounding that the person who says "But I discipline my body and bring it into subjection, lest, when I have preached to others, I myself should become disqualified" is the great teacher and preacher of the whole world St. Paul. He who had ascended to the third heaven and saw things no one has seen or heard!

BOLDNESS

Sometimes there are situations which need the wisdom of the honest servant, while other situations need a bold courageous servant. A perfect example is Elijah the Prophet rebuking Ahab the king and it all ended with Elijah being taken to heaven in a fiery chariot, while the dogs licked Ahab's blood fulfilling Elijah's words.

Same with John the Baptist who confronted Herod the king because of breaching the Law, and although the scene ended with the beheading John the Baptist, yet his voice is still echoing throughout the ages "it is not lawful for you"

All the prophets, apostles and honest servants who were delegated to pass the heavenly messages were bold and courageous, they never feared death, thus Lord Jesus said to His disciples, "And do not fear those who kill the body but cannot kill the soul. But rather fear Him who is able to destroy both soul and body in hell." (Matt.10: 28). The Lord also said to Isaiah the Prophet: "Cry aloud, spare not; Lift up your voice like a trumpet;" (Is. 58: 1), also to Ezekiel the Prophet, "And you, son of man, do not be afraid of them nor be afraid of their words… do not be afraid of their words or dismayed by their looks, though they are a rebellious house. You shall speak My words to them, whether they hear or whether they refuse, for they are rebellious." (Is. 2: 6, 7)

Had it not been for the courage of the honest servants in old, we could have lost many Christian principles and beliefs, many servants and apostles were martyred, "the souls of those who had been slain for the word of God and for the testimony which they held." (Rev.6: 9) The blood of these heroes watered the seeds of faith of Christianity and so it is flourishing and blossoming till this day.

How wonderful were the Three Saints in Babylon when Nebuchadnezzar tried to force them to worship the idol and abandon the Living God, they answered him courageously and boldly, "O Nebuchadnezzar, we have no need to answer you in this matter. If that is the case, our God whom we serve is able to deliver us from the burning fiery furnace, and He will deliver us from your hand, O king. But if not, let it be known to you, O king, that we do not serve your gods, nor will we worship the gold image which you have set up." (Dan. 3: 16-18); the result was throwing them in the burning fiery furnace yet the angel of the Lord saved them.

We can feel this boldness in the life of the Apostles and their writings; when St. Paul was warned not to go to Jerusalem because of the Jews who wanted to kill him there, he answered, "What do you mean by weeping and breaking my heart? For I am ready not only to be bound, but also to die at Jerusalem for the name of the Lord Jesus." (Acts 21: 10-13).

St. Peter also says, "And do not be afraid of their threats, nor be troubled. But sanctify the Lord God in your hearts" (1 Peter 3: 14, 15).

The honest servant should not favour or flatter anyone, it is a great sin to hide the truth if we know it, God is always supporting an honest servant, avoiding what Saul the king did when he confessed to Samuel the Prophet saying, "I have sinned, for I have transgressed the commandment of the Lord and your words, because I feared the people and obeyed their voice." (1 Sam.15: 24). So no wonder the Lord rejected him and gave the kingdom to David who always repeated, "The Lord is my light and my salvation; whom shall I fear? The Lord is the strength of my life; Of whom shall I be afraid?" (Ps.27: 1)

An honest servant should be sure that the Lord is with him, supporting and encouraging, as long as he is dwelling in the secret place of the Most High and abiding under the shadow of the Almighty. The Lord says, "Fear not, for I am with you; Be not dismayed, for I am your God. I will strengthen you, Yes, I will help you, I will uphold you with My righteous right hand." (Is. 41: 10)

THE SPIRITUAL LEADERSHIP

The spiritual leadership is a heavenly gift from God to the person who is really ready to accept it, according to his deep faith; total obedience, strong love and his sacrifice of all worldly issues for the sake of the Lord, "But what things was gain to me, these I have counted loss for Christ." (Phil.3: 7)

Joseph was a slave in Egypt in Potiphar's house, but he had favour in his master's eyes and he delegated him as the leader of his house, at the time he was a slave in the flesh, he was a free man in the spirit, and so he didn't subdue to the sin. He was imprisoned unjustly, but even in the prison he was a leader, "because the Lord was with him; and whatever he did, the Lord made it prosper." (Gen.39: 23) and even so until he became the second to Pharaoh.

St. Paul the Apostle was a captive in the ship guarded by the Roman soldiers on his way to Rome for trial before Caesar. When the sea was enraged with wind and high waves, everyone was so frightened, and here Paul acted as the leader of the group, "But after long abstinence from food, then Paul stood in the midst of them and said, "Men, you should have listened to me, and not have sailed from Crete and incurred this disaster and loss. And now I urge you to take heart, for there will be no loss of life among you, but only of the ship. For there stood by me this night an angel of the God to whom I belong and whom I serve, saying, 'Do not be afraid, Paul; you must be brought before Caesar; and indeed God has granted you all those who sail with you." (Acts 27)

Moses whom Pharaoh's daughter adopted as her son, "But when he was set out, Pharaoh's daughter took him away and brought him up as her own son. And Moses was learned in all the wisdom of the Egyptians, and was mighty in words and deeds." (Acts 7: 21,22). He wasn't granted the spiritual leadership in Pharaoh's luxury palace, but in the Sinai wilderness, "By faith Moses, when he became of age, refused to be called the son of Pharaoh's daughter, choosing rather to suffer affliction with the people of God than to enjoy the passing pleasures of sin, esteeming the reproach of Christ greater riches than the treasures in Egypt; for he looked to the reward." (Heb.11: 24-26).

Here, it is worth a comparison between Moses' attitude before being given the spiritual leadership from God and after He appeared to him in the Burning Bush. At the first we see the bodily zeal and human means, killing and burying, fear and failure; while later we see the spiritual strength and heavenly gift, the heavy tongue talking eloquently. We witness wonders and miracles and finally we see the first largest and well organised evacuation in history and then the wise and great leadership in the wilderness.

Jeremiah the Prophet was called to service during the most critical time for the children of Israel, where demonstrating religiosity, evil, wickedness and artificial worship prevailed. It wasn't easy for him to start calling in a field full of thorns, to a rotten society, and find a response from anyone!! When Jeremiah apologized, the Lord encouraged and gave him the leadership, then He touched his mouth, "Then the Lord put forth His hand and touched my mouth, and the Lord said to me: "Behold, I have put My words in your mouth. See, I have this day set you over the nations and over the kingdoms, to root out and to pull down, to destroy and to throw down, to build and to plant." (Jer.1: 9, 10)

That was exactly what God did with Elijah and John the Baptist who horrified Ahab and Herod the kings. The same with Samuel the young lad when he prophesied, and appointed David the shepherd as the King of Israel.

God has no favourtism, when He appointed these men and many others for leadership, He had foreseen their total obedience, great faith, strong love and readiness for this position. After Joshua was appointed a leader succeeding Moses, "the Lord said to Joshua, "This day I will begin to exalt you in the sight of all Israel, that they may know that, as I was with Moses, so I will be with you." (Joshua 3: 7)

The spiritual leader does not give up leadership at an old age, because there is no ageing in leadership, unless we give up our love to the Lord and His companionship.

REFRAINING FROM THE SERVICE

Reasons for refraining from the service might include:

1-   THE DESIRE OF GROWING SPIRITUALLY:

We cannot separate between a person who is growing spiritually and a person who is not, or an advancing one and another who is behind, because this growth is a companion of the spiritual life, we keep growing spiritually till we depart from this world. So, a person who refrains from the service till he is fully grown spiritually will never serve, because growth doesn't have a specific evaluation by which we can be sure that we have reached full spiritual growth.

In addition, the more we advance spiritually, the more we will discover our weaknesses and sins, so we might probably feel that we are the worst yet we have to serve the Lord, as long as we have the necessary potentials for service. At the same time, we should keep growing spiritually during our service, because this helps in our service, so we have to do both.

The lazy servant, who hid his master's talent in the ground, was not punished because he wasted the talent, but because he didn't use it to win more talents! (Matt.25 and Luke 19). So as long as the Lord has granted us special talents, we have to use them and win more souls to our

Master the Lord, or as expressed by St. Augustine: "Let's serve others with the spiritual gifts endowed on us by God".

St. Paul the great preacher wished; "For I could wish that I myself were accursed from Christ for my brethren, my countrymen according to the flesh" (Rom.9: 1-3)

As interpreted by St. John Chrysostom, 'accursed..... to the flesh' means his readiness to give up temporarily the sweet Divine negotiations with the Lord for the benefit of his brethren.

It is worth mentioning here that the service itself gives the servant growth and comfort, as written by St. Paul, "For the word of God is..... sharper than any two-edged sword." (Heb.4: 12)

How wonderful are St. Paul's words! The two-edged sword points to strength in one side and its effect on the other. The same with the word of God, it affects both sides, the one who says it (the servant) and the one who hears it (the served).

My brethren, don't think that the servant is just giving, he is taking as much as he gives. St. John Chrysostom says: "The words of the Lord Jesus are fulfilled in those who care about the salvation of others "give and you will be given". The Lord gives comfort as much as you care about your service, in addition to the fact that the service encourages us to care more about our spiritual life.

2-THE FEELING OF UNWORTHINESS:

We do not deny the honour and sublimeness of the service, and all the preparations accompanying it, as well as the huge responsibility before God, the church and our own conscience, yet we should not fear the service; "For you did not receive the spirit of bondage again to fear, but you received the Spirit of adoption by whom we cry out, "Abba, Father." (Rom.8: 15)

As human beings, with all our weaknesses we do not deserve any of God's gifts and blessings, but we have full deservedness in the Blood of our Lord Jesus the Saviour.

Pride would make us feel that we deserve any of God's gifts and grace, while feeling unworthy is a result of being a humble person and it is a factor of success in the service, on condition not to fall into despair and faint-heartedness.

After the miracle of catching the great number of fish (Luke 5), Peter felt the heaviness of his sins and his unworthiness for the Lord to come into his ship, and immediately and in humbleness "When Simon Peter saw it, he fell down at Jesus' knees, saying, "Depart from me, for I am a sinful man, O Lord!" (Luke 5: 7) and the Lord answered him, "Do not be afraid. From now on you will catch men."

So, here we find that delegating the service to Peter was a result of feeling unworthy it is very beneficial to feel our weakness sometimes; we are unworthy to pass the message of salvation to others and care for the sheep of the Good Shepherd. Yet it is wonderful to also have holy zeal towards those living astray from God, it is good to have the desire of extending the Kingdom of Christ on earth. No one is void of iniquity or sin; so we have to go in both paths at the same time: struggle in our spiritual life and in our service to others and to feel unworthy for the service and to feel the sublimeness and honour of the service. St. Paul's words are really encouraging saying: "And He said to me, "My grace is sufficient for you, for My strength is made perfect in weakness." (2 Cor.12: 9)

3-WAITING FOR THE CALL:

Some people refrain from service claiming that they haven't heard a clear invitation from God, while actually the concept of the call would be ambiguous in their minds i.e. they might think that something miraculous will happen to call them to service, or a heavenly revelation in a dream and the like.

We are not denying the possibility of such things, but there are so many other ways to hear the voice of God. It is written: "God, who at various times and in various ways spoke in time past to the fathers by the prophets, has in these last days spoken to us by His Son" (Heb.1: 1, 2). God has numerous ways to talk to us and reveal His will in our lives.

If we need to do something, the best approach is to pray, we may share with others also in prayers and attend liturgies, then if we feel really comfortable about it, that means God is approving and happy with it as long as it is not contradicting the church teachings or the Divine commandments.

When we talk about prayer and feeling comfortable, we have to give it enough time, not just a day or two then complain about praying and not hearing God's voice; especially dealing with important issues such as consecrating ourselves for the service, we should not stop praying and pleading the Lord, as well as consulting trusted spiritual leaders.

Here, we need to clarify something important; the fact that we are all called to serve, so we do not need an extraordinary power to prove it; people fall into two categories: some want to serve and some are pushed to serve.

This is clear in the life story of two prophets: When Isaiah the Prophet heard the voice of the Lord saying, "Whom shall I send, and who will go for us? He immediately answered, "Here am I, send me." (Is. 6: 8). As for Jeremiah the Prophet, he was urged to serve after telling the Lord, "Ah, Lord God! Behold, I cannot speak, for I am a youth." (Jer.1: 6)

4-FAMILY ISSUES:

Sometimes the family form a hinder for service as our Lord Jesus says, "and a man's enemies will be those of his own household.'(Matt.10: 36); and the two main branches connected to the family are the parents, wife and children.

It is very strange that getting married would be a reason to hinder the service, and here we are not objecting to the blessed matrimony, but we are talking about marriage which prevents servants from going on with their service. Marriage is supposed to be a blessing and supporter for service.

The wife could be a great blessing for the servant, as she shares life with him, she could also share the service in whatever field which suits her; Sunday School, guiding young girls, visiting the widows and needy, tailoring clothes for the poor etc. That is why it is preferable to choose a wife who would lean towards the service, and not ones to stop the service.

As for the parents, we love, honour and obey them according to the Holy Commandment, but if their love is contradicting with the love of God, we have to go ahead with the love of God, as our Lord Jesus says, "He who loves father or mother more than Me is not worthy of Me." (Matt.10: 37). Also telling His Mother when they found Him teaching at the temple, "Did you not know that I must be about My Father's business?" (Luke 2: 49). It is also written, "We ought to obey God rather than men." (Acts 5: 29)

This doesn't mean that we can't discuss this issue with our parents, for there is a solution for every problem through love and prayers, we have many examples where the parents were resisting service or consecration of their children, yet upon the faithfulness and insistence of their children they were convinced.

5-PROBLEMS OF THE SERVICE:

The nature of the service of God involves lots of hardships and problems; it is a kind of the narrow gate which all believers should deal with happily in order to reach spiritual freedom.

When the Lord Jesus sent His disciples, He sent them "like lambs amongst wolves" (Luke 10: 3). This applies exactly to the servants in the service, it is a very strange scenery to see lambs serving calmly and gently amongst the wolves, who have no authority to harm the lambs!!

Since that time, the honest servants are serving knowing that fact, as St. Paul says, "For I think that God has displayed us, the apostles, last, as men condemned to death; for we have been made a spectacle to the world, both to angels and to men. We are fools for Christ's sake, but you are wise in Christ! We are weak, but you are strong! You are distinguished, but we are dishonoured! To the present hour we both hunger and thirst and we are poorly clothed, and beaten, and homeless. And we labour, working with our own hands. Being reviled, we bless; being persecuted, we endure; being defamed, we entreat. We have been made as the filth of the world, the offscouring of all things until now." (1 Cor.4: 9-13). Again, the Apostle mentions these tribulations in 2 Corinthians Chapter 12.

So, an honest servant is the one who carries the spiritual weapons tolerating difficulties (2 Tim.2: 3).

If we put in mind that the devil always tries to hinder the spread of the kingdom of God on earth, supported by a group of evil people carrying his will, we will then understand that he is the reason for many of the problems arising during our service.

Some of these problems might include:

6-Money:

Some might refrain from going ahead with the service because of the lack of money; whether it is needed for the personal needs of the servant or for the sake of the service itself.

But as a matter of fact, money was never a problem for an honest servant; when we read the Lord Jesus' words in Matthew 6: 19-43, we notice that the Lord wants us to totally trust our Heavenly Father and so, a servant should not worry about any troubles whether he is responsible for a big family or for the congregation.

It is impossible for faith and worry to gather together, exactly as light and darkness or water and fire. If a believer has faith in the Lord Jesus trusting His promises, he can surpass all problems and fears.

The Lord Jesus never sends anyone to service while in need; "Whoever goes to war at his own expense? Who plants a vineyard and does not eat of its fruit? Or who tends a flock and does not drink of the milk of the flock?" (1 Cor. 9: 7), also, "And my God shall supply all your need according to His riches in glory by Christ Jesus." (Phil.4: 19)

When the Lord Jesus sent His disciples for elementary missions, He commanded them saying, "Carry neither money bag, knapsack, nor sandals." (Luke 10: 4). The Lord who cares for the sparrows and the birds which do not plant or reap would definitely care about His servants, "The eyes of all look expectantly to You, and You give them their food in due season. You open Your hand and satisfy the desire of every living thing." (Ps.145: 15, 16)

The Lord praised the angel of the Church of Smyrna "I know your works, tribulation, and poverty (but you are rich)" (Rev.2: 9).These words also apply to the consecrated servants.

Someone might wonder: is it a sin to live in an acceptable

life style while the burdens of our responsibilities are too many and heavy?! We are fully aware with all these issues, but we have to understand the personality of the servant and his mission. The servant is a person who finds pleasure in God's company and in delivering His holy message to others, while other people find pleasure in different fields even if they are of a good nature. The Lord says about Himself, "And my delight was with the sons of men." (Prov. 8: 31). The same with a servant, his delight is with the creation of God.

The servant should believe in the blessings bestowed upon him who serves the Lord honestly: spiritual and material blessings, good health and a blessing in whatever he touches. So the Lord compensates the servant in other ways rather than the materialistic satisfaction sought by the children of the world.

The Lord provides protection, health, happiness, inner peace...etc. Such things that could not be bought or attained by any means through money.

As for the needs of the service, we consider money a means not an aim, we read in Acts 4: 32-35 "Now the multitude of those who believed were of one heart and one soul; neither did anyone say that any of the things he possessed was his own, but they had all things in common. And with great power the apostles gave witness to the resurrection of the Lord Jesus. And great grace was upon them all. Nor was there anyone among them who lacked; for all who were possessors of lands or houses sold them, and brought the proceeds of the things that were sold, and laid them at the apostles' feet; and they distributed to each as anyone had need."

This was done due to a mere spiritual intention, because "the multitude of those who believed were of one heart and one soul; neither did anyone say that any of the things he possessed was his own, but they had all things in common."

How wonderful is this verse "and laid them at the apostles' feet".That was their attitude towards money, at the feet! An honest servant uses the money and never lets money control his life.

7-PEOPLE RESISTING THE SERVICE:

Some people might resist the service and this is a very old attitude, "the Lord will have war with Amalek from generation to generation." (Ex.17: 16). Amalek is a symbol of the devil who has followers resisting the work of God.

We have many examples in the New Testament, Elymas the sorcerer tried to withstand Paul and Barnabas in Cyprus, seeking to turn the proconsul Sergius away from the faith (Acts 13). St. Paul also writes, "Alexander the coppersmith did me much harm. May the Lord repay him according to his works. You also must beware of him, for he has greatly resisted our words" (2 Tim. 4: 14-15).

To prove the legacy of his mission to the church of Corinth, St. Paul kept recording his tribulations in spreading the word, among which were "in perils among false brethren" (2 Cor. 11: 26)

Addressing the Galatians, he also mentioned the false prophets, "And this occurred because of false brethren secretly brought in (who came in by stealth to spy out our liberty which we have in Christ Jesus, that they might bring us into bondage)," (Gal.2: 4). Also to the Corinthians, "But I will tarry in Ephesus until Pentecost. For a great and effective door has opened to me, and there are many adversaries" (1 Cor.16: 8, 9). When he talked about the final days and the hardships to take place, he writes, "But know this, that in the last days perilous times will come..... as Jannes and Jambres resisted Moses, so do these also resist the truth: men of corrupt minds, disapproved concerning the faith; but they will progress no further, for their folly will be manifest to all, as theirs also was." (2 Tim.3: 1-9)

When there are some people resisting the work of God, it is a proof that this service is successful, because Satan starts his war when there is a danger threatening him. So an honest person should be ready to face this war, as Joshua the Son of Sirach says, "Son, when you come to the service of God, stand in justice and in fear, and prepare your soul for temptation." (Joshua Son of Sirach 2:1)

The service could face resistance from within, and not necessarily from outside, this might even be more fierce and dangerous. The Lord Jesus Himself was resisted by the great scholars of Scripture; the Scribes and Pharisees!!

St. Paul the Apostle mentions that these people are brethren, but they are false brethren, "But what I do, I will also continue to do, that I may cut off the opportunity from those who desire an opportunity to be regarded just as we are in the things of which they boast. For such are false apostles, deceitful workers, transforming themselves into apostles of Christ. And no wonder! For Satan himself transforms himself into an angel of light.Therefore it is no great thing if his ministers also transform themselves into ministers of righteousness, whose end will be according to their works." (2 Cor.11: 12-15)

Yet, we have to remember the Apostle's words, "but they will progress no further, for their folly will be manifest to all, as theirs also was." (2 Tim.3: 9)

The honest servants would never abandon the service because of these resistances; otherwise the message of Jesus would not have reached us!! St. Paul says about them, "to whom we did not yield submission even for an hour, that the truth of the gospel might continue with you." (Gal.2: 5). Let's always remember St. Paul's words to his disciple Timothy, "But you be watchful in all things, endure afflictions, do the work of an evangelist, fulfill your ministry." (2 Tim.4,5). Also God's words to Joshua, "Be strong and of good courage; do not be afraid, nor be dismayed, for the Lord your God is with you wherever you go." (Joshua 1: 9)

8-THOSE WHOM WE SERVE:

There are some fields where it is hard to serve, those whom you are serving do not cope with you, and so the servants get bored and cannot feel the fruit of their service, thus giving up!! The Lord Jesus was rejected when He started His teachings at Nazareth, "Now He did not do many mighty works there because of their unbelief." (Matt.13: 58)

People respond differently to the word of God, as mentioned by the Lord Jesus at the Parable of the Sower, yet this Parable ends with "But the ones that fell on the good ground are those who, having heard the word with a noble and good heart, keep it and bear fruit with patience."(Luke 8: 15). Let's meditate in His words, "bear fruit with patience", although the ground is good, their hearts are noble and good!!

If the ground is neglected it will need lots of ploughing and digging in order to be suitable again for planting. The same with the souls, until they give the expected fruits!!

All the souls are created in the likeness of God and His image, as St. Paul says: "For every creature of God is good" (1 Tim.4: 4). When the Jews in the city of Corinth opposed Paul, "he shook his garments and said to them, "Your blood be upon your own heads; I am clean. From now on I will go to the Gentiles", yet the Lord "spoke to Paul in the night by a vision, "Do not be afraid, but speak, and do not keep silent; for I am with you, and no one will attack you to hurt you; for I have many people in this city." (Acts 28: 6-11)

Another characteristic of those whom we serve is their quick change of mind, the multitude cried out in a cheerful voice "Hosanna to the Son of David" on Palm Sunday, but five days later, they cried out "Crucify Him!!"

In Lystra, St. Paul healed a man born crippled "Now when the people saw what Paul had done, they raised their voices, saying in the Lycaonian language, "The gods have come down to us in the likeness of men!" And Barnabas they called Zeus, and Paul, Hermes, because he was the chief speaker. Then the priest of Zeus, whose temple was in front of their city, brought oxen and garlands to the gates, intending to sacrifice with the multitudes.". And the Apostles hardly convinced them not to act in such a manner.

Things were changed after a very short while, people were infuriated against St. Paul, "Then Jews from Antioch and Iconium came there; and having persuaded the multitudes, they stoned Paul and dragged him out of the city, supposing him to be dead." (Acts 14)

St. Paul highlighted this fact by saying, "I marvel that you are turning away so soon from Him who called you in the grace of Christ, to a different gospel." (Gal.1: 6)

EVERYONE IS CALLED TO SERVE

The service is not limited only to teaching; it is strongly connected to love. If love is present, then there should be a service, and if the service is successful, it is an indication that it is done with great love and holy zeal.

The first and greatest commandment in Christianity is love as our Lord says, "You shall love the Lord your God with all your heart, with all your soul, and with all your mind.' This is the first and great commandment. And the second is like it: 'You shall love your neighbour as yourself.' On these two commandments hang all the Law and the Prophets." (Matt.22: 40)

If you are a living member in the Body of Christ, you have to feel the sufferings of any member in this Body. Thus love will lead you to do something to help those in pain and that is the service! But if you cannot feel the need of the suffering, be sure that you are not a living member in Christ.

You are serving when you talk to others about God, when you visit a sick person and encourage him to pray and come closer to God, when you comfort someone in grief, when you lead someone to church and to attend spiritual meetings, when you just help any person in need or direct him to the right path. Thus we have many chances to help and show our love to God and His children.

Let's meditate in the miracle of healing the paralytic, "Then they came to Him, bringing a paralytic who was carried by four men. And when they could not come near Him because of the crowd, they uncovered the roof where He was. So when they had broken through, they let down the bed on which the paralytic was lying." (Mark 2: 3-5)

Here we have a rescue team, they were very close friends, their great love led them to this idea of uncovering the roof and letting down the bed in front of Jesus. They didn't say anything to the Lord, all what they did was bring their sick friend in front of the Life Giver and the great Healer.

Another characteristic of these friends which the Lord has revealed is "their faith", in addition to their strong will and insistence to achieve their goal.

Can't we be like these four friends? Can't we lead a paralytic soul, infected with sin and bring it to the Lord? Sin brings misery and sadness, very little would like to stay in such a state. Many people need someone to help them and take them to Jesus, like the sick man of Bethesda, when the Lord Jesus asked him, "Do you want to be made well?" He answered, 'Sir, I have no man to put me into the pool" (John 5).

Many spiritually sick people know Jesus' mercy, grace and kindness, yet they are dead in their sins and iniquities and a dead person does not have a will and cannot move. They need someone to hold their hands and help them get out of their misery, "Awake, you who sleep, arise from the dead, and Christ will give you light." (Eph.5: 14)

It was a strange message sent by Mary and Martha to the Lord Jesus, "Lord, behold, he whom You love is sick." (John 11: 3). They didn't ask for something specific, they didn't talk about their love to their brother and longing for his healing, they were quite sure that the Lord's love to Lazarus exceeded theirs.

Dear brethren; all we need to do is to pray for those sick people, mention their names and ask the Lord for their healing, ask Him to release them from the bonds of the devil.

St. John the Beloved writes, "But whoever has this world's goods, and sees his brother in need, and shuts up his heart from him, how does the love of God abide in him? (1 John 3: 17)

FROM JERUSALEM TO THE END OF THE EARTH

The Lord's commandment to His disciples before His Ascension was not to depart Jerusalem to start the service, "but to wait for the Promise of the Father.... you shall receive power when the Holy Spirit has come upon you; and you shall be witnesses to Me in Jerusalem, and in all Judea and Samaria, and to the end of the earth."(Acts 1: 4-8).

This was the last commandment from the Lord Jesus to His disciples, before being taken in a cloud to heaven. These words are very important as they form the basis for any service. He put an order for the service; first in Jerusalem, then Judea, then Samaria till they reach the end of the earth preaching the good news of salvation.

First: In Jerusalem:

The Lord ordered His disciples not to depart Jerusalem, and to witness for Him there. Jerusalem is considered the city of the Great King, where the Temple exists. It denotes the heart and the holy spiritual life of a human being, considering him a temple of the Lord. Witnessing to Christ in Jerusalem means to witness to Him through my life and my holy deeds.

Many people do not follow the order set by our Lord, and they try to witness in Samaria or the end of the earth before witnessing for Him in Jerusalem. Here, they start experiencing mistakes and failure! Our Master Christ reminds me to witness for Him in Jerusalem first, because the good news of salvation came out from Jerusalem, and out of your holy private life the blessings will reach others and be beneficial for them.

Jerusalem was the most important city for the Jews, there was the Temple where they offer sacrifices, and so it was the cornerstone of their worship and pilgrimage. The same with your inner Jerusalem, everyone looks at you as a servant, they glorify our Father in Heaven through you. As for you, you have to continuously offer thanksgiving offerings from pure lips.

Why do we have to start with Jerusalem? It is the smallest area where we can witness for the Lord, if we do well, then we deserve to start witnessing for Him outside it, and we will get power from the Lord. The Lord commanded His disciples to wait for the descent of the Holy Spirit. He wants us to serve through the power of His Spirit and how mistaken people can be when they think they can serve depending on their power, wisdom and eloquence. The disciples gained this power in the Upper Room, while pouring themselves in prayers, in one accord, in a locked room waiting for the Promise of The Father. The same with us, we will not gain this power unless we are in an Upper Room; i.e. when we are lifted above the worldly matters and lust, pouring ourselves and waiting for the work of God within us, after closing the doors and windows of our senses, and in this spiritual upper room the Lord will reveal Himself, as He used to appear to His disciples, encouraging and filling them with His Holy Spirit. With this power,

Peter who denied the Lord in front of the maid, witnessed for Jesus Christ before thousands of Jews and with the same power we can serve the Lord till the end of the earth, because we are powered and led by the same Spirit.

Second: In All Judea:

The Jews are the children of Christ, to whom He came and they rejected. So witnessing in Judea is the service offered in the house for the family and the small circle in which we live. It is worth highlighting the words "in all Judea". Sometimes people often neglect the service in this field, which consequently causes many problems and hardships in the service.

Joshua the Son of Nun says, "But as for me and my house, we will serve the Lord." (Joshua 24: 15). Also, "But if anyone does not provide for his own, and especially for those of his household, he has denied the faith and is worse than an unbeliever."(1 Tim.5: 8), and, "one who rules his own house well, having his children in submission with all reverence (for if a man does not know how to rule his own house, how will he take care of the church of God?)" (1 Tim.3: 4,5)

The apostle considers caring for the house is the measurement of the service, for if a servant cannot look after his own household how could he care for the church??

Third: In Samaria:

The worship of the Samaritans was a mix between Judaism and Paganism, thus witnessing in Samaria represents our service amidst the divert believers and the non-believers.

So, after establishing his own spiritual life and witnessing to Christ through his holy deeds in Jerusalem and all of Judea, a servant can start serving in a field which needs a lot of toil and tolerance. Service in Samaria needs love, mercy and consideration of emotions. When the city of Samaria rejected Christ, James and John said, "Lord, do You want us to command fire to come down from heaven and consume them, just as Elijah did?" But He turned and rebuked them, and said, "You do not know what manner of spirit you are of. For the Son of Man did not come to destroy men's lives but to save them." And they went to another village." (Luke 9: 51-56)

In addition to tender feelings, a servant serving in this field needs to have deeper studies and research concerning those whom he is serving. It is a hard field, yet the faith of just one person might be a reason for the salvation of the whole city, as what had happened with the Samaritan woman.

Fourth: To the End of the Earth:

How wonderful when the word of God is growing and spreading, "How beautiful are the feet of those who preach the gospel of peace who bring glad tidings of good things!"(Rom.10: 15)

How happy would a servant be when he heads to remote areas carrying the glad tidings of salvation to people living there, whom he never saw or contacted before.

CONCLUSION

Finally, we would like to advise our dear servants not to judge matters according to their outer appearance, or just consider one point of view. We should be aware with all the church's needs. We should not just be zealous for the service – although this is required - but we have to be empowered with the strength of the Lord and the Promise of The Father.

No matter how we toil and serve, we should always remember that the harvest is plentiful but the labourers are few. We have to believe that the Lord is working within us and through us. Let's have a self- account and review our principals in the service, let's start anew in strong faith and will.